Rome Florence Discovery

An easy, breezy guide to the most interesting restaurants, shops, sightseeing, and other attractions in Rome and Florence

Features *Rome/Florence Discovery* Courtesy Card for exclusive privileges and special discounts

by John Alexander and Marianne Friedland

E. P. Dutton & Co., Inc. | New York

Copyright © 1970 by Discoveries Overseas, Inc.
All rights reserved. Printed in the U.S.A.
First Edition

No part of this publication may be reproduced or transmitted in any form or by any means, electronic or mechanical, including photocopy, recording, or any information storage and retrieval system now known or to be invented, without permission in writing from the publisher, except by a reviewer who wishes to quote brief passages in connection with a review written for inclusion in a magazine, newspaper or broadcast.

Published simultaneously in Canada by
Clarke, Irwin & Company Limited, Toronto and Vancouver

Library of Congress Catalog Card Number: 79–115931

Contents

How We Picked Our Places	5
So This Is Rome 11 So This Is Florence	17
Museums, Churches, and Ruins	21
How to Be a Part-Time Native	30
Where to Eat: Restaurant Discoveries	37
Where to Buy Clothing and Accessories:	
Shopping Discoveries	71
What to Bring Home: More Shopping Discoveries	107
For the Collector: Art and Antiques	129
You Never Looked Better: Personal Care	139
Rome After Dark: Nightclubs	151
Looking Around and Getting Around	159
Finding a Good Hotel	168
What to Know Before You Go	
"How Much Is That, Anyway?"	175
Who and How to Tip	175
"But Will It Fit?"	176
"What's It Like Outside?"	178
The Holidays of Italy	178
What to Do in Case of Emergency	179
Crossing the Language Barrier	180
How to Use *Rome/Florence Discovery*	182
Maps	184–187
Index	189

How We Picked Our Places

It's no coincidence that the words "Rome" and "romantic" have the same origin. For Rome *is* romantic, with every quality that the word implies—happy, friendly, colorful, nostalgic, and memorable.

But Rome can also be confusing: it is big and fast-paced, and there is a language barrier. So once you're there, where do you go? What do you do? How do you sort out, from the hundreds of sights to see and the thousands of places to eat or shop, those parts of Rome that will mean the most to *you?*

The best way, of course, is to ask a friend who lives in Rome. But most travelers, unfortunately, don't form any Roman friendships until nearly the end of their stay—if, indeed, they form any at all. And that's a shame, because one knowledgeable Roman is worth a thousand books, and a few personal tips are more valuable than a long list of places.

Everything that is true of Rome is equally true of Florence.

If, however, you have some insight into these cities in advance; if you know what Romans and Florentines do in their spare time and can join them as a participant rather than watch them as a tourist; and if you know where they themselves eat, shop, and have fun—then instead of feeling bewildered, you'll feel at home.

The purpose of *Rome/Florence Discovery* is just that—to make you feel at home in Rome and Florence.

Over the course of time, and after several trips to Europe together with our mates, we have met a number of Romans and Florentines whose knowledge of their cities has greatly enhanced the pleasure of our visits. When we wanted to know what to see, we asked them. When we wanted to know where to eat, we asked them. When we wanted to know where to shop, we asked them. And their answers—in Rome and Florence alike—were often quite different from the standard guidebook answers. For instead of suggesting the well-known places on the well-traveled tourist track, our Roman and Florentine associates directed us to the restaurants where *they* eat and the shops where *they* shop.

These places became the nucleus of *Rome/Florence Discovery.*

The 92 establishments and services described here in detail are not the most famous or expensive. But all are of outstanding quality, and all share an eagerness to serve you.

In that, they are representative of many thousands of other establishments in Rome and Florence. Patronized mostly by Romans and Florentines, they are—for travelers—true "discoveries."

Moreover, each establishment included here has agreed to offer a special courtesy to travelers who come to them on our recommendation. The restaurants and clubs will make you feel at home with *una cortesia,* a gracious gesture which may be a before-dinner drink *(aperitivo),* an after-dinner drink *(digestivo),* wine, or even a dessert. Other types of establishments are pleased to offer you a courtesy discount by way of saying "Thanks for coming."

But quality, not discounts, was the basis for all our selections. None of the recommended establishments has paid a single cent to be included in *Rome/Florence Discovery.* None were—or will be—asked to.

In order to receive your *cortesia* or discount, simply detach the *Rome/Florence* Courtesy Card from inside the back cover of the book, sign it, and present it at the establishment. In restaurants and clubs, show it when you're seated; elsewhere, at the time you receive your bill. (It might also be a good idea if you jotted your passport number down on the back of the Card, as a convenience to shops which require such information when making out a bill of sale.)

Prices indicated in *Rome/Florence Discovery* are, of course, subject to change without notice. But where they appear, they are *full* prices, before your discount is subtracted.

We come now to what is every author's greatest pleasure —the privilege of giving public thanks to people who contributed to the birth of the book.

Acknowledgment must certainly be made to our mates— Jerry Friedland and Lily Alexander, who researched the Eternal City on foot and in libraries before turning to the roles of editors, critics, and manuscript-readers.

Credit must also go to our "team" in Italy itself. In Rome, to Signora Elda Villa, whose wide knowledge of shops and fashions proved invaluable, and to Paul Suttman, an American sculptor living in Rome, who with his wife Elisse introduced us to fine galleries and restaurants. In Florence, to Mrs. Lo Ullman, an editor of one of Italy's top magazines of leather fashions, and to Signora Carlotta Fagiuoli, who knows the shops of her city backwards and forwards.

The major portion of our gratitude, however, is reserved for Jouni Lilja, veteran Rome-based correspondent for European newspaper, television, and radio services. Finnish by birth, he studied in Germany, taught in Switzerland, speaks nine languages, and knows practically everyone in Italy worth knowing. Jouni's interest, and his willingness to place his wide circle of contacts at our disposal, have made *Rome/Florence Discovery* possible.

                John Alexander and Marianne Friedland

So This Is Rome

So This Is Florence

So This Is Rome

For nearly the span of human memory travelers have come to Rome.

Suppliant vassals sailed to Ostia, the port of Rome, in long-oared galleys laden with tribute. Barbarian horsemen clattered down upon the decaying Imperium. Medieval pilgrims approached on foot to worship at the shrines of Christendom. Gentlemen of the Enlightenment arrived, first by carriage and later by ship and train, to broaden their education. Modern tourists swoop down in screaming jet liners to see the splendid ruins.

Rome has survived them all.

Throughout the ages, foreigners have looked to Rome as a special place. Not even its foes could resist it. Many of the Goths who came as plunderers stayed as settlers. The Frankish kings were so enamored of Rome that they called their domains the Holy Roman Empire (although it was neither Holy, nor Roman, nor an Empire). Napoleon was so proud of the city that, although he named his brothers kings of Naples, Holland, and Westphalia, he named his *son* the King of *Rome*. The Germans came in 1943 as allies and were viewed as conquerors. The Americans came in 1944 as conquerors and were welcomed as liberators.

Rome has survived them all.

Heathens, barbarians, pilgrims, scholars, artists, writers, poets, soldiers, adventurers—all came to absorb the city in one way or another. Yet, in one way or another, Rome absorbed *them*. For it is more than an eternal city. It is a city which is all things to all people.

Consider some of the things it is.

It is one of the most religious cities in the world, and surrounds the home office of the Roman Catholic Church. Yet it is also one of the most pagan cities in the world, the city where *"la dolce vita"* was born and named.

Its chaotic politics have given it a reputation for anarchy, yet its designers and artists and film-makers have made it a synonym for creativity.

It is a city with international flair, a mecca for the sophisticated and cosmopolitan, yet it retains a disturbingly provincial quality, and its people can be noisy and argumentative.

Like a gigantic stage on which the props keep changing, Rome at one moment enchants and stimulates, and the next moment angers and frustrates.

And what of the Romans themselves? What of the people who live in this sprawling, colorful city half as old as time? What are they like?

If ever there was a city with a personal character, a city whose people were predictable in their very unpredictability, it is Rome. To the marrow of their bones Romans display a vivid and passionate love of life. They love pretty women, fine music, good food, soccer, spectacle, their wives and children and parents and sisters and brothers and aunts and uncles and cousins, and thumbing their noses at authority—not necessarily in that order but all with equal ferocity.

No one yields to the Roman when it comes to admiration for pretty women. Though his reputation as a "pincher" is somewhat unfair, he will follow a beautiful woman for blocks just to tell her how beautiful she is. If she accepts the gambit —well and good. If not, it is all the same—there are other beauties to be flattered in a city where Gina Lollobrigida, Sophia Loren, Claudia Cardinale, and Vera Lisa started.

Today's Roman is well-dressed, well-shod, and well-fed. Also he is thinner than he was a few years ago, which is, paradoxically, a sign of prosperity. It's easy to remember when the typical Roman was on the chubby side, not just because he ate so much *pasta* but also because, in a country where semi-starvation was a fact of life, a plump wife meant that the husband was a good provider and a plump husband meant that the wife was a good cook.

Today, many Romans are very well-off indeed. True, there is still plenty of poverty, and Italian poverty can be appalling beyond belief. But not in 2000 years has the average Roman had it so good. Shops that not long ago were dependent on tourists for survival now happily sell their wares to their fellow countrymen, and younger Romans are among the best-dressed men and women in Europe.

Cars tell even more of the story. There are 1,400,000 automobiles registered in the Rome area, nearly one for every two Romans, and 600,000 of them enter the center of the city every day. To the visitor, in fact, it sometimes seems that all the Romans are inside their little Fiat cars driving around at the same time. And the cars are frequently filled to overflowing, because Roman families—in fact, Italian families—stick together.

No one has ever described the role of the family better than Signor Luigi Barzini in *The Italians:* "Scholars have always recognized the Italian family as the only fundamental institution in the country." He terms it the source of power, the rallying point of everybody's first loyalty, the "stronghold in a hostile land. No Italian who has a family is ever alone."

There is good reason for this. Italy lay for centuries under the rule of one foreign conqueror after another. In between, it was under the domination of large landholding families and the Church. All this convinced the Italian that the only institution on which one could fully depend was one's own family.

In Rome, therefore, family loyalty pervades everything—business, social life, even one's attitude toward the government. (There is always at least one member of the family who belongs to the opposition party, so that when it becomes the party in power, the influence of the family will remain intact.) A Roman family takes care of its own.

With so much energy devoted to respect for family, it isn't surprising that a Roman's respect for outside authority is virtually nil. The family as an institution is venerable and solid, while the laws and statutes of the city and country are an ever-changing jumble. It takes no great effort to disregard them. In fact, one of the nation's leading economists has calculated that if all the taxes on the statute books were collected, they would absorb 110 percent of national income.

But there is no danger of that. Romans make a game of avoiding the tax collector, and frequently win it, so the commune of Rome (or the SPQR—Senate and People of Rome—as it is officially called) is constantly in debt to the tune of hundreds of millions of lire. In 1968, for example, the University of Rome remained closed for months because there was no money to pay for faculty housing.

Perhaps money to keep the bureaucracy from floundering could be raised if there were industry to pay the taxes. But although Italy has since the war become the seventh largest industrial power in the world, the huge plants are all in the North—around Milan and Turin. There is no heavy industry worth mentioning in Rome.

That being the case, it's fair to ask where the bulk of Rome's affluence comes from. In one way or another, from two prime sources—tourism and the movies.

About 25 million foreigners a year visit Italy, and at least 60 percent of them pass through Rome. The money they bring with them keeps the restaurants and shops, nightclubs and small factories functioning nicely. But not much of it finds its way into the coffers of SPQR.

The other industry is perhaps a little more considerate of the commune as a whole, probably because it is more centralized and easier to keep track of. Rome is rapidly becoming the new Hollywood of the western world. If you find that every restaurateur or shopkeeper you visit tells you that his clientele includes movie and television stars, it's not just a line cooked up for visitors—it's probably true. Over 10,000 actors and actresses are registered with Rome's theatrical agencies, and the Rome studio of Dino de Laurentis is the most modern film-making facility in the world. What's more, many American movie companies have taken to filming in Rome, because facilities are better, the weather is more consistent, and wages are lower than they are back home in Hollywood. Even many "westerns" are now the product of Rome studios, and more than one new cowboy star endorses his paychecks with an Italian name.

Rome's rise in the world of make-believe is hardly a surprise. Romans are born actors, anyway. They attack life as though they were onstage—with animation and flair, fully hoping and usually believing that all eyes are on them. To a Roman, it's important to see and to be seen, and above all, to express oneself. That accounts for all the violent gesticulating of the hands, dramatic rolling of the eyes, vibrating highs and throbbing lows in the voice—Romans are constantly bubbling over with vigor and intensity, constantly on parade.

You'll discover this the moment you arrive. You'll be caught up in the ceaseless commotion and gaiety of Roman streets. You'll see soldiers, priests, peasants, pretty girls, would-be celebrities hoping to attract attention by hiding behind smoked glasses, *paparazzi* with their everpresent cameras rushing around looking for real celebrities to photograph, people sliding into and out of little cars, people springing onto and off of tiny motor scooters—the whole panorama filled with the color and vitality of an opera by Verdi or Puccini.

If you visit Rome for any length of time, however, chances are you'll wake up one morning and find the hyperthyroid streets practically deserted, the volatile Romans almost nowhere to be found. Maybe the telephone won't be working or the elevator won't be running. Maybe there won't be any waiters when you go to breakfast, any buses running when you leave the hotel, any store clerks in attendance when you begin your day's shopping. Then it will dawn on you—a strike has been called.

Rome—all of Italy, in fact—is continually plagued by strikes, and Italian strikes are unlike any other. *Reason 1:* Italy has only been industrialized since the 1950's, and the workers now feel that it's time they got theirs. *Reason 2:* Italian unions are weak, without the financial resources to support a long strike. They therefore walk out sporadically, usually for only one or two days at a time. Happily, their intentions are always announced in advance, so Romans simply shrug their shoulders and make the best of it. You should do the same. After all, that's Italy.

We've discovered, however, that many visitors completely misinterpret Italian strikes. They think that because Italians strike regularly, and frequently vote the Communist ticket, the country is in danger of going Communist. That's not too likely. Italy's Catholic traditions run too deep. People may *talk* Communist but, as recent elections indicate, when the chips are down a majority *vote* Catholic.

The Holy Roman Church is, after all, headquartered in the midst of Rome. In the Vatican City, to be exact. The Vatican is an independent state within a city, by virtue of Mussolini's concordat with Pope Pius XI in 1929. But it is the smallest independent state in the world, about ¼ mile square, and its population is only 1200. Yet it has all the amenities necessary to sustain life.

The Vatican has a hotel. It has a daily newspaper (in which all the ads are printed in Latin). It issues its own stamps and its own money (which looks exactly like ordinary lire except that the bills carry the face of the Pope instead of the usual imprinting). It has its own supermarket. It also has a coffee bar where you can relax with coffee and drinks.

Of its full-time population, just over 400 are citizens of the Vatican itself. There are 27 cardinals, 27 archbishops, 54 members of the Swiss Guard, 154 gendarmes, and 148 civilians. All must be home every morning by 11 P.M., or be locked out for the night.

The Vatican even has a mayor, but he doubles as the Bishop of Rome and Primate of Italy. Who else but the Pope himself? He often appears in the window of St. Peter's on Sunday at high noon to bless the crowd. The piazza below him is thronged with the faithful. A Papal appearance has all the electric excitement of Saturday afternoon before the football game back home. There's a vibrating feel of anticipation in the air. You have to experience it to fully comprehend it.

As important a link to the Roman past as the Church is, there is a tie which is even more firm. It is the character of the people themselves. All Romans throughout the ages have had one quality in common—the ability to be happy, by being realistic and making the best of what they have. To be happy is an art, and it is the quality of happiness which attracts people to Rome. Paris has better food, London has (for Americans, at any rate) more nostalgic sightseeing, but Rome has happiness. The word *simpatico* is an Italian word, a word much used in Rome, and while it is actually untranslatable, one could come close with "warmth and humanness." *Simpatico*—warm and human—sums up the Roman character.

Perhaps this is why, over the years, so many foreigners have been drawn to Rome. For the Roman is friendly and accepting. He takes you for what you are, not who you are—except when it comes to dealing with you on an official level. Then, however, he may even treat you better than he would a fellow Roman. We well remember parking our car illegally one day and, upon returning to it, finding a piece of paper tucked under the windshield wiper. Oh, oh, we thought, one involuntary run-in with foreign officialdom coming up. But no. It was not a traffic ticket; it was a message, printed in five languages, and this is what it said:

Dear Sir:

Rome is happy to welcome you among the visitors to the city.

It sometimes happens that even the most careful driver infringes, without meaning to, the rules of the road. In the instance, you have failed to observe the rule contained in Article —.

The Communal authorities are quite convinced that this infringement was unintentional, and we wish you a happy stay.

The Mayor

Simpatico.

So This Is Florence

Rome and Florence are like two different worlds. The people look the same, speak the same language, and eat basically the same foods. But there the similiarities end. The differences between Rome and Folrence are not just in size and appearance; they're differences in kind.

Rome is a large international city; Florence is a small Italian city.

Rome is an ancient city with great ruins; Florence is a medieval city with great art.

Rome is a city of high fashion, fine restaurants, and easygoing ways. Florence is a city of high enterprise, fine craftsmanship, and businesslike efficiency.

In Rome, 11 P.M. is the heart of the evening, time to be eating dinner in a busy restaurant or looking forward to several more hours in coffee bars and nightclubs. In Florence, 11 P.M. is the time to close up the town and be home in bed, because tomorrow is a working day.

If you remember Florence from shortly after the war in 1946, or even from shortly before the flood in 1966, you wouldn't recognize that quiet, charming little city today. It's a thriving commercial center, bursting with vitality—though not too busy to pause every so often and appreciate its jewel-like setting in the Tuscan hills and its stunning collection of art treasures.

Florentines take immense satisfaction in their cultural heritage. Though the average Florentine hasn't time to visit museums every day, he puts them on the agenda for out-of-town guests; though opera and concerts are no more a Florentine's daily fare than a Roman's, he nevertheless supports them and tries to attend frequently.

For Florence, while it has certainly gone commercial, has not gone commercial in a bad sense. In fact, Florence is the only city in the world which still raises generations of artisans on a large scale. It is as natural for the son of a Florentine leather worker or goldsmith to follow in his father's and grandfather's footsteps as it is for him to occupy their home or pray in their church. If two words could be used to summarize Florence, those words would be *commerce* and *continuity*.

You'll acquire a good sense of both if you come to Florence from the South—from Rome. Most of the way, you'll be passing through scenic farmlands and hilly countryside.

lovely mist-covered valleys, and blue-green vistas that remind you of paintings you've seen somewhere but can't place. Then, suddenly, Florence bursts upon you and everything changes.

You're in a city whose high medieval buildings lean out over the stone walkways almost far enough to touch, where the narrow medieval streets seem all to go one way—the wrong way from the direction you want to go—and are all clotted with cars. Wherever you look, there's frantic activity—people shopping, people working, people selling, buyers from the United States ordering Florentine crafts to sell back home. The energy is everywhere.

Immense pride in workmanship, intense channeling of a vast quantity of talent—this is Florence's inheritance from centuries gone before. What Florentine artisans do, they do with genuine skill and great enthusiasm. What they do not do, unfortunately, is the magnificent original work of their ancestors—but then, no people anywhere do what the Florentines' ancestors did. Florence in the years between 1350 and 1600 produced a concentration of genius that has never been duplicated since: the Renaissance.

Count off the names of the great Florentines.

In the arts: such immortal painters as Giotto di Bondone, Fra Angelico, and Michelangelo Buonarroti, who was also the greatest sculptor who ever lived.

In literature: Dante Alighieri, one of the most sublime poets of all time.

In science: Galileo Galilei, the astronomer who changed man's concept of the world and its place in the universe.

In artisanship: the superb goldsmith Benvenuto Cellini.

In government: Niccoló Machiavelli, whose name is still a synonym for crafty statesmanship.

The entire family of Medici: Cosimo, the financier; Lorenzo the Magnificent, statesman and patron of the arts; Giulio, who became Pope Clement VII; and Cosimo the Great, Duke of Florence and Grand Duke of Tuscany.

And towering over them all, casting a giant shadow across the most creative era in human history, the man who defies categorization because he was all at once artist, scholar, scientist, inventor, sculptor, architect, and engineer, the man for all times and all seasons—Leonardo da Vinci.

That all of these geniuses should have flourished during one short span of time in one small city in the hills of northern Italy staggers the imagination. Yet it happened. You can stand today in the Church of Santa Croce, north of the

Arno River, and be surrounded by the tombs of Michelangelo, Galileo, and Machiavelli.

That the works of these men of genius survived, were saved for our generation, is due in large measure to the Medici, who cared about and strongly supported the arts. That these works may be saved for future generations—if indeed they are—will be due mostly to luck. For Florence in 1966 was drowned by more than six feet of mud and water when a dam suddenly broke and the Arno River overflowed its banks. Priceless works of art displayed on the ground floor of churches and museums, or stored in their basements, were permanently destroyed or seriously damaged. An irreplaceable collection of ancient books and manuscripts in the basement of the National Library was forever ruined.

But the moment the floods receded, the Florentines began to rebuild their shops and homes. Muck and mire were shoveled out into the piazzas and hauled away. Craftsmen went to work with stone and marble and traditional Florentine skill to recreate their city.

As for the art and the books—the Florentines apparently felt that since the entire world claimed ownership, the entire world would help to take on the burden of rescuing and cleaning up what could be saved. That is, in fact, what happened. With shovels and mops and tender loving care, people from all over the world descended on Florence for the massive recovery job. The great Ghiberti panel from the door of the Baptistery was plucked from the mire, millions of water-logged pages of rare books were laid out in the sun to dry, and while the world wept over the loss of the marvelous Cimabue crucifix, the Florentines wryly noted that at least the outdoor statues in the elegant Piazza della Signoria had been partially cleansed by the flood—and went back to work.

Today, much of Florence has been totally rebuilt. Its face has been changed. There are shiny new goldsmith shops on the ancient Ponte Vecchio. There are sparkling coffee bars designed to look exactly like the ones that were washed away. There are elegant leather boutiques whose décor is more Parisian than Florentine.

But the conditions which caused the Arno to overflow that November night in 1966—a combination of heavy rains and winds and mud slides—have not been corrected, even though dikes could be built and the waters diverted. For something to be done, someone would have to pay—and who that someone should be has not been resolved. The Florentines, characteristically, shrug the problem off, noting that the 1966 flood occurred 100 years to the day after the last great flood—the implication being that they are now safe for another 100 years.

Meantime, the paintings are again in place on the church and museum walls, and what is not displayed is neatly stored away in the basements. Trade is brisk along the Tornabuoni, and the leather and ceramics workshops are booming.

Florence is back in business.

Museums, Churches, and Ruins

It happens so often, and not just to first-time travelers. Someone plans for years in order to go to Rome. At last the great day comes when he buys his tickets, gets hotel reservations, and, filled with excitement and enthusiasm, picks up some guidebooks and begins to map out what he'll see.

Boom! The bubble bursts!

There are so many things to see. There is so much ground to cover. And every time he mentions that he's going to Rome, someone tells him "Be sure to go to such-and-such" or "Don't miss so-and-so." Yet he knows he can never see it all.

Of course he can't! No one can and no one ever does. Rome is so huge that not even a native Roman ever covers all of it.

Now let's talk about you.

The things you should do in Rome are the things *you* want to do. If you'd like to take every sightseeing tour in town, do it. But if you want to go shopping every day or spend every evening in a nightclub, do that instead. Don't feel that you have to keep pushing ahead for one more museum, one more church, one more statue or set of ruins. One more isn't worth it. The pressure to cram everything in is probably greater in Rome (and Florence) than anywhere else, but if you're not the museum-exploring type back home, or the type who visits churches for the sake of their architecture or stained glass, don't try to become one in Italy. You'll only grow bored. And that is the worst mistake of all. So see a few things well rather than many on the run. You'll appreciate them more, remember them better, and in the end have a more enjoyable trip.

How to See Rome

Let's start with how you should *not* go about seeing Rome. You should not plan a special visit to something you're going to see anyway. For example, if you plan to do some shopping on the Via Condotti, don't waste half a morning going to the Spanish Steps, because you'll see them anyway while you're shopping. If you intend to attend an open-air opera in the Baths of Caracalla, you can skip the Baths on your walking tour. If you decide to stop for coffee or ice cream, stop near Piazza Navona and see the Bernini fountains while you're eating your *gelato* or drinking your *espresso.* If you particularly want to see a special church, and you happen to be Catholic, go to Mass there on Sunday. (If you're not Catholic, find out what else is along the way, and see the church en route.)

The point is that some sights deserve a great deal of time and attention, while others can merely be "skimmed." And face it—some will just have to be skipped altogether, in order to spare time for other activities that can spell the difference between a trip to remember and a trip to forget as quickly as possible.

Yet, if you plan your sightseeing sensibly, covering Rome strictly as time and energy permit, you can skim plenty of cream off that lovely surface in just a few days.

To begin, we'd like to suggest **a walking tour of the ruins.** With the possible exception of Athens, Rome has the most awe-inspiring ruins in Europe. The grandeur that was ancient Rome has never completely disappeared.

Start with the Roman and Imperial Forums, in the heart of modern Rome near Piazza Venezia. But first, go behind the Piazza's massive Victor Emmanuel monument and up the Michelangelo stairs to the Piazza del Campidoglio. Head across to the middle of the three buildings facing you. This is the Senatorial Palace, and from the gardens on either side of it, you'll have a bird's-eye view of both the Roman and Imperial Forums, spread out in front of you like a map. Then descend to the Roman Forum itself.

In its heyday, this was the commercial, religious, and political center of the entire Roman Empire. Walk along the Sacra Via, where Mark Antony delivered his historic eulogy to Julius Caesar, in front of the ruins of buildings which witnessed Caesar's assassination. Here were the House and Temple of the Vestal Virgins, the Basilica of Julia, built by Caesar himself, and the Temple of Saturn, which housed the Roman treasury. Here, too, are ruins of the Temple of the Divine Caesar, built by command of Augustus, and, surprisingly unmarked by the passing centuries, the still-splendid Arch of Septimius Severus, erected in 202 A.D. by the Senate and People of Rome.

Walking the grassy spaces and worn footstones of the Forum, where once the Sacra Via ran, you come at last to the Piazzale del Colosseo, the Great Square of the Colosseum, hard by the Arch of Constantine, the great Emperor who forced Christianity upon the Romans and, by doing so, altered the history of the world for all time. Now one of the busiest squares in Rome, the Piazzale displays only two ruins of what stood here during Imperial times. Yet what stupendous ruins they are—the Arch itself and that vast hulk known as the Colosseum.

Begun by the Emperor Vespasian sometime between 70 and 75 A.D., and inaugurated by his son Titus in 80 A.D. with a celebration which lasted for more than three months, the Colosseum was a cavernous labyrinth of corridors, passages, storerooms, even cages for wild animals (which were brought up to the arena floor through an elaborate system of trapdoors and pulleys). What did the ancient Romans think of all the public money that was poured into construction of a 50,000-seat stadium? They loved it, for Nero had taken its site for his private garden, and the Romans welcomed the return of the area to public use. Did it then become a place where Christians and barbarians battled each other and wild animals for the fateful thumbs-up signal of the paying customers, or is that only a legend? No one really knows. But standing in this immense arena, whose only animals today are hordes of semi-wild cats, it is easy to close one's eyes and smell the stench of combat, hear the roar of the crowds.

Coming out of the Colosseum, you're only a short walk from the Baths of Caracalla on Via delle Terme. Once upon a time, they were the site of mass bathing by ancient Romans, who luxuriated in steam rooms, cold rooms, massage rooms, and swimming pools which would do credit to the most elegant modern health club. Still filled with exquisite 2000-year-old mosaics (which are kept in a constant state of repair), the Baths can easily be reached from the Piazzale del Colosseo.

Even if your visit to Rome is a short one, you'll have to spend **an entire day in the Vatican.** Not just a nation within a city, not just the world headquarters of the Roman Catholic Church, it is the site of one of the most memorable churches and museums ever built. The church, of course, is St. Peter's, and you approach it best on foot, walking across St. Peter's Square against the counterpoint of the great Bernini columns which encircle it. So beautifully proportioned is the church itself that it doesn't appear to be the largest church on earth. Yet as you approach, it seems to grow before your very eyes, assuming a size and dignity that are overwhelming.

Inside, you again meet masterpieces by Bernini, including his monumental Baldachino above the High Altar. Ninety-five feet high and cast of bronze taken from the pagan Pantheon, it is directly under the vast vaulted dome of the church itself.

Within St. Peter's are some of the most moving paintings and sculptures in the world, but none surpasses Michelangelo's Pietà, luminous marble figures of the dead Christ held in the arms of the Virgin Mary. From the church, visit the Vatican grottoes, underground tombs of the Popes, and then ascend to the dome itself for a breathtaking view of the Eternal City.

After this, we'd suggest a coffee break, at the Vatican's own coffee bar. Then you can tackle the Museum.

The Vatican Museum has nearly 500 paintings by most of the great Italian masters, a collection of antiquities which contains the largest forest of ancient sculptures ever gathered under one roof, and the incredible Vatican Library, a storehouse of books and manuscripts so enormous that it has never been fully catalogued. It would be foolhardy for us to attempt in this short space to try to describe the contents of the Vatican Museum. All we can do is urge you to buy a book on the spot, to study it, and not to try to see everything. Visit, if you can, the roomful of Raphaels and see the sculptures "Apollo Belvedere" and "Laöcoon." Otherwise, we would say this: if you had just two hours in Rome and time to see but one thing, it should be the Sistine Chapel.

Michelangelo spent four years lying practically flat on his back, painting the story of Genesis from the Creation to the life of Noah, and twenty years later he returned to finish the job by depicting The Last Judgment on the Altar wall. His monumental achievement is as near to perfection as anything a human being has ever done. In a sense, it is itself a miracle. But seeing it sometimes poses a problem, because the Chapel is small and the tourists are many. If you can manage it, get there about 9 A.M., when the Vatican doors are opened, and don't waste any time getting up the spiral staircase to the Chapel itself. If luck is with you, you may have a few moments almost to yourself before the human wave rolls in.

Having roamed the Roman ruins and visited the Vatican, what else should you do? You should perhaps **drive out of Rome,** down the ancient Appian Way to the Roman catacombs there. Begun about 312 B.C. and still in use, the Appian Way was in ancient times a highway along which the wealthy built both villas for the living and tombs for the dead. Today, it has again become a fashionable area for the villas of Roman socialites and movie stars. Of the ancient structures, few remain—notably the Tomb of Cecilia Metella, daughter-in-law of the triumvir Crassus, who died about 100 B.C.

The entire countryside out the Appian Way is honeycombed with catacombs, subterranean burying grounds for the early and much-persecuted Christians. At one point, Christians actually held religious services in the catacombs, in an effort to hide their activities from Imperial spies. To this day, in the area, you'll see ancient Roman walls and patches of highway still paved with the original stones. But the catacombs are the Appian Way's main attraction, and most are clearly marked.

Among the more unusual are the Catacombs of St. Calixta, a murky maze of underground tunnels with apertures for corpses six deep on either side of the corridors. Vases, plates, urns, and other household utensils were placed with the dead, and when a passage was filled, it was simply sealed up and another passage was hollowed out. Many of the passages are dimly lit with naked electric bulbs, but watch where you're coming from in any case. A catacomb is a grim place to get lost in—and it's easy to do!

Another worthwhile side trip is the one which leads you east of Rome toward Tivoli and the famed Villa d'Este. En route, you'll pass Hadrian's Villa, constructed by the Emperor Hadrian during the first century A.D. as a retirement community for himself and a pleasure palace for his thousands of hangers-on. Ruined though they now are, the homes, theaters, baths, and libraries give you an excellent idea of the luxury in which some Romans lived. Our suggestion would be to take along some bread, sausage, and wine, and have a picnic lunch in this pleasant greenery where Hadrian's court once indulged in Roman feasts.

After Hadrian's Villa, you continue on to Tivoli and Villa d'Este, an Italian rival to the splendors of Versailles. Cardinal Ippolito D'Este, a most sybaritic gentleman, fashioned it about 1550, and the elegant terraces, dazzling fountains, and exquisite landscaping must indeed have created a pleasant atmosphere in which to live.

Now all of these and many more—the Panthéon, Hadrian's Tomb (Castel Sant'Angelo), Villa Borghese (see "How to Be a Part-Time Native"), to touch upon just a few—are well worth seeing. But some of Rome's lesser-known sights are equally interesting.

Consider the church of Santa Maria della Concezione, near the Via Veneto, an above-ground cemetery where the skeletons of long-dead Capuchin monks line the walls, and the chandeliers and wall decorations are fashioned from ribs, bones, and vertebrae.

Consider the Capitoline Museum with its haunting collection of Etruscan relics. The Etruscans preceded the ancient Romans along the banks of the Tiber, and left behind as their legacy a fascinating assortment of wall paintings, bronzes, and ceramics. There is no lack of Etruscan objects in the Rome area, and they clearly demonstrate that these mysterious people had, in the misty past, created a highly developed civilization. But who they were, where they came from, what language they spoke, and what eventually happened to them—these are questions that no one can answer.

How to See Florence

It is 249 kilometers from Rome to Florence on the *autostrada*, about 154 miles. Yet the journey is measured not in distance but in centuries. In the four hours that it takes to drive from the Roman kneecap to the Florentine thigh of the Italian boot, you pass as if by time machine from ancient times to the Renaissance, from one epoch in human history to another.

Florence—*Firenze*, it is called in Italian—was the cradle of the Renaissance. And the great Florentines—all of them: Michelangelo, Machiavelli, Giotto, the Ghiberti brothers, the family of the Medici, Galileo, and the miraculous Leonardo da Vinci (a Florentine by adoption)—all left their indelible marks upon the city.

When you see Florence today, it doesn't look much different than it did to them. The Ponte Vecchio, despite war and flood, still bridges the Arno as it has ever since 1345, and it is still lined with goldsmiths' shops, still a center of the jewelry trade. The green, white, and pink cathedral, called Il Duomo, second largest church in the world, still dominates the Florentine skyline as it has for almost 700 years. The Baptistery, whose stupefying East Door, executed in bronze by Lorenzo Ghiberti and named the Gate of Paradise by Michelangelo himself, has stood as a lesson in genius since the twelfth century. And that exquisite bell tower, the Campanile, remains unchanged since Giotto himself designed it in 1334. For a small city, with fewer than 500,000 people, Florence is a glorious example of beauty and grace.

Perhaps because of its magnificence, it has to be *felt* to

be appreciated. You cannot just "do" Florence. For even if you could see its great architecture on the run, so to speak, you would miss what is equally awe-inspiring, the incomparable paintings and sculptures with which the city is blessed. To see them any other way than carefully is to create a monstrous blur in your mind and plant the seed for a lasting regret.

There is a method, however, which can give you enough varied experiences to hold your attention, while seeing the city at a sensible pace. Follow it, and you won't miss much. Figure to take a minimum of three days, and you'll be able to see most of what Florence has to show.

On the **first day,** go to Duomo, sometimes (but not often) known by its official title, Cathedral of Santa Maria del Fiore. Notice especially the intricate and beautifully colored façade (which dates only from the late nineteenth century), the ingenious cupola designed by Brunelleschi, and the breathtaking stained glass windows created by artists like Donatello and Ghiberti. Go then to nearby Giotto's Tower, his *campanile,* and if you have the energy, walk up the 414 steps to the summit, from which you see an enchanting medieval panorama of the entire city. Then visit the Baptistery and the Duomo Museum.

After lunch, taxi across the Arno River to the Pitti Palace, built in the mid-fifteenth century by the proud Florentine merchant Luca Pitti to show one Cosimo de Medici that he, and not Cosimo, ranked first among the Florentines. Stung, Cosimo within the decade broke both the power and the wealth of the Pittis, but their *palazzo* still stands, facing the green splendor of the Boboli Gardens. Vast it is, with over 500 paintings in the famed Palatine Gallery alone (not to mention the Gallery of Modern Art, the Silver Museum, or the Royal Apartments), and you cannot hope to see it all. So, unless you specifically want to visit the other sections, confine your tour to the Palatine Gallery and pay special attention to the works of Titian, Rubens, Raphael, del Sarto, Velasquez, and Ghirlandajo, masters of the Italian, French, and Spanish Renaissance. The Palatine Gallery occupies the entire north wing of the *palazzo,* and should keep you totally absorbed for most of the afternoon.

If there's time and you're still inclined, walk through the Boboli Gardens behind the Pitti Palace. Or visit Cascine Park—a two-mile-long stretch of trees and flowers—for an old-fashioned horse-and-carriage ride.

The morning of your **second day,** see the Medici-Riccardi

Palace, Cosimo's classically designed reply to Luca Pitti. A splendid example of Renaissance architecture, it contains the jewel-like Medici Chapel, a vaulted gallery frescoed by Giordano, and the Medici Museum with its paintings of that noble family itself.

From the palace, walk the block and a half up Via Cavour and east to Via Ricasoli, where you'll come to the Accademia. Here, you'll see one of the most moving works ever created by man, Michelangelo's almost-living statue of David. Here, too, you'll see many fine paintings.

Following lunch, visit the Church of Santa Maria Novella, across from the railroad station. An interesting architectural meld of Gothic, Romanesque, and Renaissance styles, it boasts stunning frescoes by Masaccio, Ghirlandajo, and Filippo Lippi, as well as the Spanish Chapel, one of the most lavishly decorated rooms in existence. Spend the balance of the afternoon "up the hill," in the ancient town of Fiesole, 20 minutes from Piazza San Marco (by the number 7 trolley).

To reach Fiesole, your trolley climbs a winding road, flanked by rows of cypress trees and luxurious homes, to a crest from which the entire Tuscan Valley stretches like a living Renaissance landscape. From this point, Florence gleams like a jewel in the afternoon sunshine, but it is neither the panorama of Florence nor the view of the Valley that makes Fiesole so worthwhile. For this city was founded by the Etruscans, some seven centuries before Christ, and the Etruscan ruins—walls, part of a gate, and a few artifacts in a museum—provide a brief and tantalizing glimpse of an entire civilization vanished into the mists of time.

Begin your **third day** in the Piazza della Signoria, one of the most dramatic outdoor statuary galleries in the world. Here stand copies of Michelangelo's David and Donatello's Marzocco, the lion which symbolizes the Florentine Republic, as well as the original of Donatello's defiant Hebrew warrior-prophetess Judith and Giambologna's statue of Cosimo I on horseback. When you stop and think whom these statues represent, you cannot help but reflect that the entire Piazza is a monument to the concept of human freedom, and it was in fact here in 1498 that Savonarola was hanged and burned for daring to oppose the power of the Medici. Every year, on the anniversary of his death, the spot where he was executed is covered with flowers.

Facing the Piazza della Signoria is the Palazzo Vecchio, ancestral home of the Medici family. As a home, it was probably uncomfortable beyond belief, but as a museum it is one family's monument to its own importance. Room after room and gallery after gallery are filled with portraits of members of the clan, and works of art by Michelangelo, Ghirlandajo, Vasari, and Bronzino abound. But don't linger too long here, because you're about to visit one of the world's greatest museums, the Uffizi Galleries, and you'll want to leave plenty of time for that.

Started in 1560 by the Medici themselves, the Uffizi contains 38 separate rooms filled with such art treasures as to beggar belief and virtually defy description. We can only mention a few:

Room II: Giotto and Cimabue; *Rooms VII and VIII:* Fra Angelico and Filippo Lippi; *Rooms IX, X, and XI:* almost exclusively Botticelli, including, in Room X, his world-famous "Birth of Venus"; *Rooms XV and XVI:* works by Leonardo da Vinci; *Room XXIII:* Correggio; *Room XXV:* Michelangelo and Raphael; *Room XXVII:* Rembrandt; and *Room XXVIII:* Titian, Veronese, Tintoretto, and Caravaggio. The museum is open daily except Monday from 9:30 A.M. to 4:30 P.M., Sunday until 1 P.M. Admission is free.

After the Uffizi, anything should be an anticlimax, yet how can you skip the Bargello? You can't, not if you want to see one more superb collection of Donatello and Michelangelo sculptures. Between armor and tapestries, carpets and carvings, the Bargello would in any other city be the most striking museum in town. It's pretty great even in Florence—and it does have all those Michelangelos: a Brutus, a Madonna, and yet another David. You'll never have a better chance than now, so go—right after lunch!

Concluding Florence, visit the Church of Santa Croce— for the art, including excellent Giotto frescoes, and for the tombs: Michelangelo, Machiavelli, Galileo, Rossini, Cherubini, and both Ghibertis. Lord Byron called Santa Croce "the Westminster Abbey of Italy." It is.

Your visit to Florence ended, you may now be turning back to Rome for the plane that will fly you home, or perhaps heading on to France or up into Switzerland. Behind you in Italy, in Rome and Florence, you'll be leaving an uncountable number of marvels yet unseen and things-to-do yet undone. May we make one last suggestion?

Before you leave Rome, stop for a moment beside the Fountain of Trevi and toss a penny into the water. For there is a legend that if you throw a coin into the fountain, you will someday return.

How to Be a Part-Time Native

Rome invites you to play along. To walk wide-eyed with awe among its ruins. To scream your lungs out at its ferocious soccer games. To rub elbows with its citizens in their coffee bars. To stay up half the night dining and drinking and dancing. To walk its streets at any hour in safety.

Rome invites you to savor the pleasures of being a Roman.

In many ways, it's easier to go native in Rome than anywhere else in Europe. For Romans more than most Europeans constantly use their famed tourist attractions—they stroll arm-in-arm through the ruins of the Imperial Forum, worship daily in churches like the ornate Basilica of St. John Lateran, where the skulls of Sts. Peter and Paul are interred, go to the opera in the ancient Baths of Caracalla, live in beautifully furnished apartments behind the crumbling façades of centuries-old buildings in the Trastevere section, drive daily past the vast ruined Colosseum.

So simply by walking around Rome as a tourist, you're already well on the way to becoming a part-time Roman.

For Romans are walkers. They walk everywhere. You should walk, too.

You might start with a short hike from the Piazza Venezia, which Romans use as a reference point for getting around. Go up the Via de Fori Imperiali, or through the ancient Forum itself, to the Colosseum. You'll see most of what remains of the Rome of the Caesars. (See section entitled "Museums, Churches, and Ruins.")

Or, from the same starting point, head up behind the Panthéon, cross the Via del Corso, and continue up Via Umiltà till you reach the Fountain of Trevi. Then retrace your steps to the Corso, turn right, and walk to Largo Goldoni. Turn right again up Via Condotti, past shops and galleries, to Piazza di Spagna and the Spanish Steps.

Another day, take a cab to the Tiber, across from Castel Sant'Angelo (Hadrian's Tomb), cross the bridge on foot, and walk up Via della Conciliazione to St. Peter's Square—directly into the teeth of the Bernini columns that circle the piazza.

Or taxi instead to the Borghese Gardens, one of the most beautiful public gardens in all the world. Aside from the Borghese Galleries, there's no special place to go—just stroll at random, watching the kids play sandlot soccer or tag under the pines of Rome.

On Sunday morning early, take a cab to Porta Portese, the sprawling Roman flea market in Trastevere. Here, under umbrella-shaded stalls, you can buy virtually anything imaginable. Be prepared to bargain, however, because prices are three times higher than they should be, and haggling is expected. If you don't like to bargain, don't buy at all. But it isn't difficult, and once you accomplish it, you'll have the delicious feeling of doing what Romans do.

There are a couple of other tricks to feeling like a Roman. One is to sit down frequently, on a park bench or at an outdoor coffee bar, and take time to absorb the view. Maybe it's the marvelous panorama of the city seen from the Janiculum Hill, across the Tiber, when the late afternoon sun bathes Rome in a reddish-gold light. Maybe it's a children's puppet show in progress in a park. Whatever it is, take the time to absorb it. Don't just dash through.

The final secret of seeing Rome? Don't look at ruins and see only ruins. Try to imagine them in their prime. Are you in the Forum? Then picture in your mind's eye not shattered marble façades and once-graceful columns lying broken on the ground, but the living place that was the Sacra Via— busy government buildings and bustling markets and temples. Are you in the Colosseum? Try to see not a jagged mass etched against the sky but a giant stadium filled with fans who shout as loudly and root as vigorously as people at this year's Lions-Saints game—bearing in mind that those ancient fans may well have been rooting for *real* lions or *real* saints!

But why confine yourself to *imagining* what a Roman spectacle was like? Go see one for yourself. We'd suggest a soccer game. For sheer excitement and bloodthirsty partisanship, nothing surpasses soccer in Italy. The word "fan" comes from the Italian word for "fanatic," and on any Sunday afternoon from September to May, a visit to Rome's Olympic Stadium or Florence's Municipal Stadium will show you why.

Italian soccer fans *are* fanatics. They're crazy. A soccer game in Italy is not just a game; it's a test of will, an affair of honor, a struggle between mortal enemies. Has the home team scored?—the stands rock with cheers. Has the visiting team scored?—then honor has been besmirched. Has the local star been roughed up?—it's all a Roman or Florentine can do (and sometimes more than he can do) to keep from rushing down on the field to avenge his hero!

Not all Roman spectacles evoke as much passion as soccer,

however. During the summer, you can take in an opera in the Baths of Caracalla or an outdoor concert in the Stadium of Domitian on the Palatine Hill—good examples, by the way, of how Romans put ancient ruins to modern use. (Florentines go to operas or concerts inside the 2800-person Communale on Sundays between October and April, or at the Boboli Gardens during the summer.)

Another great Roman spectacle is—the movies! Romans love going out to be entertained, and movies, as both fantasy and escape, appeal to their sense of the dramatic. So if some evening you're worn out from eating or touring or nightclubbing, you'll be doing a very Roman thing if you take a couple of hours out for the *cinema*.

After the movie—in fact, at almost any hour the spirit moves you—join your fellow Romans at a coffee bar, that very peculiar institution created especially for the pace of Italian life.

Consider the coffee bar's uses:

It's a place to get a cup of *espresso* (coffee steam-filtered and sipped black) or a *cappuccino* (coffee with hot milk whipped in), a quick snack or delicious pastry, an *aperitivo* (before-dinner drink) or *digestivo* (after-dinner drink), even a brandy or Scotch and soda.

It's a place to meet friends or business associates, have a nightcap after dinner or another cup of coffee (because it's only 1 A.M. and too early to go to bed), or just sit or stand and watch the people.

Romans also use coffee bars as human refueling stations. Since they're up and on the job by 8 or 9 in the morning, and rarely get to sleep before 1 or 2 the next morning, they pour countless cups of high-octane coffee into the tank just to stay awake.

The bars keep the same long hours their clients do. Most are busy early in the morning and then again by 11 A.M., as hungry Romans gulp the day's second cup and wolf down a pastry. (All that most of them had for breakfast was a roll and first cup of coffee, and lunch is still several hours away.) After that, people continue in and out all day long. The tempo reaches its peak after 11 P.M., when dinner is over and socializing begins in earnest.

Many coffee bars have a special type of clientele—movie stars, dowagers, truck drivers, even people waiting to catch a bus. As a part-time Roman, you'll soon discover your own favorite(s). But to get you started, here are a few of ours:

In Rome:

Antico Caffè Greco, Via Condotti 86. Just a few doors

from the Spanish Steps, it's popular with shoppers. Bar and three rooms of tables. You'll be served by elderly waiters in white tie and tails.

Tre Scalini, Piazza Navona 28. In summer you can sit outdoors and gaze at the lovely Bernini Fountain in the closed-to-traffic piazza. Serves some of the best ice cream in Rome. Ask for Gelato Tartufo.

Pasticceria Rosati, Piazza del Popolo. After-dinner hangout for fashionable Romans and movie people. Serves delicious pastries.

La Tazza d'Oro, Via Orpani across from the Panthéon. Coffee, not conversation, comes first here. You drink it standing up or leaning against the sacks of coffee that line the walls.

In Florence:

The Black Bar, Via Calzione 107R, across from the Duomo. Mostly for young people, it's the staging area for Florentine swingers. The coffee bar is downstairs, tables upstairs (facing the Duomo).

Rivoire, Piazza della Signoria, has the best hot chocolate in Florence.

Bar La Borsa, Via Porta Santa Maria 55R. You sit outdoors but under cover. Ice cream is the specialty.

At most coffee bars, you may drink standing up at the bar or be served at a table. To be served at a bar you must pay the nearby cashier first and then present your receipt to the barman. At the table, the cost per cup is higher. Never, never pay for your coffee at the bar and then take it to a table—that violates all the rules.

Like all people, Romans keep life interesting by switching pastimes. Simply fall in step with what's happening when you arrive. During the summer, swimming is popular at several beaches near Rome. Ostia (Lido di Roma) is closest, but frequently overcrowded. Santa Marinella is fashionable, but stony. Ladispoli is sandy but a bit run-down. Anzio, famous as an Allied beachhead during World War II, is about the best. It's 60 kilometers (36 miles) south of Rome.

Horse racing draws big crowds, too, in Rome and Florence alike. Thoroughbreds race at Rome's Campanelle track monthly except December, January, and April. In Florence, either thoroughbreds or trotters are off and running at Cascine Park all year round.

It's not love of good horseflesh that brings Italians out to the races, however—it's the thrill of the race, which mixes so well with the volatile Italian personality. When it comes to animals, an Italian's—or at least a Roman's—first love is cats. There are about 400,000 wild cats in Rome, and you see them everywhere—chasing scraps of paper in the wind, sunning themselves on monuments, resting comfortably on coils of construction wire or fallen columns in the ruins. The Colosseum is filled with them. So is the Imperial Forum. Hundreds of cats throng the Largo Argentina, near the Campi di Fiori market. No one would think of harming them. When a campaign was launched to get rid of them, Romans rose in wrath. "Rome," they said, *"belongs* to the cats." So the cats subsist very well. Every morning, you'll see little old ladies feeding their favorite broods—usually with yesterday's spaghetti!

Romans love their cats, because cats are as independent and unregimented as Romans themselves, but children are Rome's treasure. You see these kids at their best on Sunday in the Borghese Gardens, out walking with the family. Probably the most elegantly dressed youngsters in the world, adored and doted on, they're uninhibited, spontaneous, and a delight to watch. Yet they somehow manage to be polite and well-mannered.

The longer you spend in Rome, the more you'll realize that the qualities which distinguish Roman children apply equally to Roman adults. They, too, are uninhibited and spontaneous, with the happy faculty of enjoying small pleasures with large enthusiasm. And once you're imbued with their city—once you become a part-time native—their huge capacity for loving life will never completely leave you.

Where to Eat: Restaurant Discoveries

The Restaurants

The food of Rome is the mirror of Italy. Colorful, boldly flavored, distinctive, imaginative—all the brilliant qualities of this kaleidoscopic peninsula are captured on the plates of one cosmopolitan city. Although variety is the keynote to Roman eating, Rome's native cuisine has certain characteristics as distinctive as that of Bologna or Sicily.

Italians are great fish-eaters. Living as they do on that long, thin boot that cuts into the Mediterranean, they habitually eat some of the tastiest fish and seafood in the world, and have developed literally hundreds of exciting ways to prepare it.

Italians are enormous consumers of veal and poultry, and their beef is regarded by many gourmets as the world's best.

Italy is the largest producer of rice in Europe, and rice dishes are almost as common in the Italian diet as *pasta*.

Italian ice creams—*gelati*, they're called—are so famous that even their names are copied the world over. (Neapolitan, spumoni, and biscuit Tortoni are only three examples.)

Whatever the dish, from whatever part of the country it comes, you're going to find it in Rome. For Rome is the point to which all roads lead, and its thousands of restaurants present a true cross section of Italian cooking. Because of its geographical location and its cosmopolitan nature, Rome is not just the political capital but the culinary center of the country, as well. And because Romans exercise the option of changing regional dishes to suit their own tastes, they often come up with delicious variations. So it's probably easier to find a truly good place to eat in Rome than a truly bad one. Perhaps the best Roman restaurants never quite scale the shining heights of glory attained by Paris's famed "temples of gastronomy," but Rome's lesser eating establishments never sink to the abysmal depths of a really bad French *bistro*, either.

Like all Italians, Romans and Florentines take their eating seriously, demanding and getting both quantity and quality. Atmosphere is fine—nobody objects to it—but what you pay for is what's on your plates, not what's on the walls.

Frequently, however, confusion arises over three terms for eating establishments—*ristorante, trattoria,* and *osteria.* Once upon a time, these terms coincided with actual differences between the types of establishment, with *ristorante* being the most elegant, *trattoria* a working-class eating place, and *osteria* (inn) the humblest. Today these terms have become completely meaningless, describing nothing more than the ambitions of the *proprietario*. Knowledgeable Romans and Florentines eat in all three types of establishment, using the quality of the food as their only criterion for selection.

Basically, a Roman or Florentine meal consists of three courses. The first is *zuppa* (soup) or *pasta* (noodles) in its myriad forms. The second is *carne* (meat) or *pesce* (fish). The third is dessert or cheese. At dinnertime, the soup or *pasta* is sometimes preceded by *antipasto* (appetizers), and you're offered both dessert *and* cheese. But no place at any time offers *pasta* as the main course, and no one ever orders it as such—that would be like walking into a restaurant in New York and ordering shrimp cocktail as your whole meal. It simply isn't done. So if the size of the *pasta* course overwhelms you, just skip it altogether and go directly to the main dish—or else order a *mezzo* portion, which is supposed to be half the size of the regular *pasta* course but is still of gallant proportions.

Incidentally, your *Discovery cortesia* in Roman and Florentine restaurants is based on the assumption that you order at least three courses, for Italians are justifiably proud of their cooking prowess and want you to experience a wide range of their culinary talents.

The Prices

In most Roman or Florentine restaurants, you'll find it difficult to pay more than $7 or $8 per person, and it's entirely possible to enjoy a perfectly delicious meal for as little as $2 or $3. In *Rome/Florence Discovery,* we have indicated the approximate cost in each recommended establishment, and have also categorized each restaurant as expensive, moderate, or inexpensive by Italian standards. Generally speaking, here's what those terms mean:

Expensive: Over $6.00 (approximately 3700 lire)
Moderate: $4.50 to $6.00 (2800 to 3700 lire)
Inexpensive: Under $4.50 (about 2800 lire)

These prices include wine, service (*servizio*), and that peculiar Italian institution called *copèrto,* a form of seating charge which appears on the menu in every eating establishment, however humble. A *copèrto* may be as low as 15 lire or as high as 450 lire, but it's a nationally accepted and perfectly legitimate charge.

The Food

What kind of food will you find in Italian restaurants? You'll frequently start with *antipasto*, a choice assortment of sausages, olives, marinated vegetables such as mushrooms and artichoke hearts, anchovies, sardines, tuna, eggs —in short, whatever the *proprietario* deems most likely to enhance the reputation of his house. *Antipasto* is not to be taken lightly: it is carefully thought out to provide you with a wide range of flavors and textures. In most restaurants, you'll be brought *antipasto assortito*, which simply means that the food is already on the plate. Some establishments prefer that you make your own selections from the *antipasto al carrèllo*, and wheel out a huge variety of *antipasti* on a cart. Given a choice, one should always stipulate *al carrèllo*.

After the *antipasto* comes the *pasta*—obviously. This is, let it be understood, the cornerstone of Italian cooking, but it is not, as so many non-Italians think, the heart of Italian cuisine. Far from it. It is only the overture to the *òpera*.

At its most basic, *pasta* is just noodles made of a flour and water dough, sometimes with eggs added. Essentially bland in taste, it gets its character from the way it is shaped—we know of some 60 or 70 different shapes—and its flavor from the sauces which are used to liven it up. In Rome, *pasta* assumes virtually every form found anywhere on the entire Italian peninsula.

Consider, for instance, the Bolognese *tagliatelle*, a flat, ribbon-like *pasta*. Prepared with butter and Parmesan cheese, and presented as *fettucine al burro*, it has been a source of fame and riches for more than one Roman restaurant.

Also from the North comes *cannelloni Bolognese*, thin squares of pasta rolled around a stuffing of finely minced meat.

And then there's *gnocchi*—little dumplings—which are usually made with potato and flour, but, when *alla Romana*, are composed of flour alone.

Southern contributions to Roman *pasta*-lovers include *maccheroni alla ciociara*, served with a sauce containing ham, sausage, and bacon, and *spaghetti a cacio e pepe*, served with the local cheese (*cacio*) and pepper (*pepe*).

Rome also has a typical soup, called *stracciatella*—the Itaian version of Chinese egg-drop soup. "Little rags," as the soup is nicknamed, is made by scrambling together eggs, flour, and grated Parmesan cheese, and pouring the mixture into a boiling broth *(bròdo)*. Though inexpensive and thoroughly commonplace, it can only be prepared on demand, which gives you some idea of the personal attention all orders receive in Italian restaurants.

If ever any city anywhere had its own "municipal dish," Rome has. It is called *abbacchio*—suckling lamb. We have seldom been in a Roman restaurant where it didn't appear on the menu. *Abbacchio* is a spring and early summer specialty which comes in virtually every form, but the most popular is surely *abbacchio arrosto*, lamb roasted in an oven or outdoors on an open spit, usually with a seasoning of rosemary. Popular variations include *abbacchio alla cacciatora* (lamb in a sauce of anchovies, olive oil, vinegar, and garlic), *abbacchio brodettato* (small pieces of lamb prepared in an egg-yolk and lemon-juice sauce), and *costoletta a scottadito* (grilled baby lamb chops).

Almost as prevalent as *abbacchio* is that famed staple of Italian-American restaurants, *saltimbocca alla Romana* (ham and veal slices in butter and white wine sauce). *Osso buco*, the wine-braised shank bone of an ox served on a bed of rice, is another Roman specialty (which comes originally from Lombardy); the marrow, spooned out from the bone, is considered by Italians to be quite a delicacy.

Vegetables, too, benefit from Roman culinary imagination. *Carciòfi alla giudèo* (artichokes Jewish-style) is an example, as are *broccoli alla Romana* and *funghi arrostiti*. The *carciòfi*, small artichokes flattened and deep-fried in olive oil, apparently originated in the tiny restaurants of Rome's ancient ghetto near the banks of the Tiber, and are well worth sampling. The broccoli, flavored with garlic, is cooked in white wine and olive oil. The mushrooms are broiled in olive oil and accented with garlic and parsley.

If all this sounds simply delicious, but the time comes when you're just too full to attack another enormous Italian meal, Roman custom thoughtfully provides a graceful alternative—an omelet, rarely on the menu but available everywhere. In place of your meat or fish order, ask for *omelette simplice* (plain), *omelette con funghi* (with mushrooms), or *omelette con prosciutto* (with ham). You can then, if you wish, proceed to the dessert, satisfied that you have eaten wisely and confident that you have chosen respectfully.

Italians, especially in Rome, stand with the French, Austrians, and Danes on the highest plateau of dessert-makers. What could be tastier (or more calorific) than *zuppa inglese* (rum-saturated custard cake), *deliziosa* (a super-fabulous-fantastic-colossal concoction of whipped cream and meringue with the flavor of almonds), or *cassata* (a Sicilian-descended fruit cake flavored with liqueur and covered with chocolate frosting)? If you like rich, sweet, fancy desserts, you can go out of your mind in Italy. Yet, as a conterbalance to all the rich and heavy foods that come before, Italians often finish a meal with delicious ice cream *(gelato)*, light and tangy water ice *(granita)*, simple fruit *(frutta)*, or cheese *(formaggio)*. Fruit, by the way, is eaten with knife and fork, not with the fingers.

Florence, not being the center of a nation but only of a region, offers a narrower range of foods than does Rome. Yet it benefits from being in the heart of Tuscany, long the stronghold of fine and distinctive Italian cuisine.

Unlike most other Italians, Florentines are not big on seasonings. Very finicky about the choice of their meat, poultry, seafood, or vegetables, they tend to specialize in heightening rather than disguising the natural flavor of the food. So the term *alla Fiorentina*, which to the world usually means "with spinach" (Florentine spinach is famous), to a Florentine means food prepared with elegant simplicity.

In Florence, for instance, beans—plain white beans known as *fagioli*—are a staple of the menu. You'll see them everywhere on the *lista*, starting right out with *zuppa di fagioli* and *minestrone*, a bean-filled vegetable soup which is not generally Italian at all but is very specifically Florentine (the Romans have, as you might imagine, adopted and adapted it).

We suspect that if you're a steak-eater, you may even prefer Forentine cuisine to Roman, because Florentines truly have a way with steaks. For one thing, they choose their cuts from magnificent Chiana steers, prized for flavor and tenderness throughout the peninsula. For another, *bistecca alla Fiorentina* (sirloin) and *costata alla Fiorentina* (rib steak) are usually grilled over an open charcoal fire, then seasoned simply with olive oil, salt, and pepper. (Backyard barbecue experts please note.)

Among the other Florentine specialties which we particularly enjoy are *arista alla Fiorentina*, lightly seasoned and slowly roasted pork loin, and *pollo alla diavola*, broiled chicken seasoned with a rather piquant butter sauce. Most menus also feature *trippa alla Fiorentina*, stewed tripe. The Florentines love it. Will *you?* All we can say is what used to be said in the Army: "forwarded without recommendation."

In Florence as in Rome, wine accompanies most meals, and is frequently included with the *prèzzo fisso* (fixed price) or an all-inclusive lunch or dinner. But Italians often drink bottled water with their meals, usually *acqua minerale* or *acqua naturale*. Don't be embarrassed about asking for it. Or ask for *birra* if you prefer—Beroni and Prinz-Brau are two of Italy's biggest-selling beers. After dinner, it's customary to sip a cup of *espresso*, and in Rome this is often done not in the restaurant but at a coffee bar. (See "How to Be a Part-Time Native.")

While cuisine may differ from one region of Italy to another, one thing remains the same—the absolute freshness of the food itself. Italy, as a relatively poor country whose people have always lived close to the soil, never found the need for a highly developed canning or freezing industry. Even today, when supermarkets selling preserved foods are gaining in popularity, most Italian restaurateurs—and housewives, too—go to market daily, buying only what is both fresh and seasonal. So the colors are sharp and the flavors are keen, tomatoes are red and broccoli's green.

One thing is sure—if it isn't fresh, Italians won't buy or serve it.

The Wines

Italian wines are much better than they're usually given credit for being. Unfortunately, Italy is so close to France that its local wines sometimes suffer by comparison. Yet even cultivated *tastevins* can find words of praise for the product of Italian grapes.

Each region has its own special *vino*, which is usually cheap and if not great at least good. In Rome, the local house wine is usually a sturdy white *Frascati*, often from the nearby hill country called *Castelli Romani*. In Florence, the house wine is frequently *Chianti Classico*, a splendidly dry wine which comes in a tall bottle.

Among the better reds are Valpolicella and Barolo. The preferred whites are Orvieto and Soave. Don't worry too much about the vintage—it isn't as important as with French wines. In any case, the dates on Italian wines are not controlled by the government—as they are in France—so the date is more often a reflection of the bottler's whimsy than the actual year of vintage. Except for the reds mentioned above, which improve with age, Italian wines ought to be drunk when they're still young. (One difficulty with Italian wines in the United States is that they're sometimes too old, but back home in Italy, close to the source, this is rarely a problem.)

While Italians, like everyone else, regard French champagne as the proper wine with which to celebrate the birth of a son, they actually have a very good champagne-like wine of their own—*Lacrima Christi:* "tears of Christ." They also have a delicious and sparkling white dessert wine, *Asti Spumante,* which is slightly sweet and a perfect mate for fruit or pastry.

The main thing is not to worry too much about the wines. In a good restaurant, order the *vino apperto*—wine of the house—which is poured directly from cask to flask, or the local specialty, which is usually bottled.

Before or after dinner, try an Italian *aperitivo* such as Campari, Punt-E-Mes, or a sweet vermouth. After dinner, an Italian *digestivo,* possibly licorice-flavored *Sambuca* or yellow, sweet *Strega,* is excellent. For the courageous, there's nothing like the fiery mountain brandy *Grappa*—repeat: *nothing* like it!

And if after *aperitivo, antipasto, pasta, saltimbocca* or *osso buco, insalata, legumi,* dessert, *vino, caffè,* and *digestivo,* you still feel the need of something else, drink a *Fernet-Branca*—the bitterest, most unappealing, most completely effective stomach-settler that we've ever tried.

Ristorante Passetto

Via Zandarelli 14
Rome
Telephone: 650–569 or 653–696 (reservations a must)

Open for lunch and dinner daily except Sunday
La cortesia: Choice of *aperitivo* or *digestivo*
Expensive

Passetto is one of the great restaurants of Europe. Founded in 1870, it enjoys an unblushing reputation for excellence, and is constantly being "rediscovered" by Roman nobility, government ministers, industrialists, and connoisseurs.

Yet for all this, Passetto's appearance is nothing to write home about—just several pleasantly decorated rooms of average size, and a *terrazza* where you eat during the summer. In the presence of the restaurant's distinguished clientele, everything about the place grows more elegant.

Where Passetto truly shines, however, is in its food—monumental. To make things easy on yourself, ask for the English-language menu, which is not a *menu touristique* but simply an English translation of the regular *lista*. But start by ordering something not on the menu at all—*insalata alla Passetto* (an exquisite salad of truffles or wild mushrooms, celery, and Gruyère cheese). Or start with *cannelloni Passetto* (tender crepes stuffed with finely chopped meat and lathered with béchamel cream).

As your main dish, turn either to *Veal chop à la Passetto* (veal, mushrooms, capers, and tomato sauce baked in a bag) or *Veal scaloppine Passetto* (veal stuffed with ham and cheese). But keep an eye out for the splendid seasonal dishes of the house.

In winter, turkey and pork are specialties, as are tiny birds about the size of your hand, which are brought to you grilled whole with the heads still on (delicious, once you get used to the idea). During spring, look for the thin, delicate asparagus.

Fall is wild game season—wild boar in sweet-and-sour sauce, roast pheasant with orange sauce, quail roasted on a spit, hare in red wine sauce, and partridge.

For dessert, try the *Monte Bianco* (chestnut and whipped cream cake) or *orange Passetto* (fresh oranges, pineapple, and peaches in maraschino liqueur). Special winter desserts are *mòro sanguinella* (blood oranges in sugar and wine) and *deliziosa* (a marvelous crushed-almond torte). During the summer, try *fragoline,* tiny wild strawberries that are indescribably sweet.

It all adds up to about 5000 lire ($8) per person, not too much for one of the most memorable of Roman meals, enjoyed in the presence of some of the noblest Romans of them all.

Ristorante La Cisterna

Via della Cisterna 13, Trastevere
Rome
Telephone: 582–543 (reservations important)

Open daily except Tuesday from 1:00 P.M. till after Midnight
La cortesia: Any drink of your choice
Expensive

Rome about 1700 is the setting for this splendid cellar *ristorante* in old Trastevere. It is in fact typical of Roman restaurants of that era, situated in a large "cave" underground, where all the guests are seated together at long tables.

No one seems to know exactly when La Cisterna first opened, although guesses range as far back as 200 years ago. Rome, despite its long history, is considerably more lax than we are about keeping records of deeds and similar transactions. But the restaurant has been under the present management since 1930, and was a favorite spot of the poet Trilussa, who in 1938 celebrated Hitler's visit to Mussolini with a cutting couplet:

> *Roma de travertino, refatta de cartone,*
> *Saluta l'imbianchino, suo prossimo padrone.*
> (Rome of Marble, rebuilt in cardboard,
> Salutes the housepainter, its next master.)

Trilussa still visits La Cisterna in spirit every night, when guests order *bocconcini alla Trilussa* (veal "tidbits" in a special sauce).

Among the other specialties of the *casa* are *agnolotti alla Trasteverina* (ravioli-like *pasta* filled with meat and served in a tomato sauce) and *pollo alla diavola* (a type of deviled chicken, served highly seasoned). Whatever you order, accent it with a light and dry red or white wine from La Cisterna's own vineyards outside Rome, in the region known as Castelli Romani.

Entertainment is modest at La Cisterna, but charming in its very simplicity. There is a small orchestra with a singer who specializes in Roman and Neapolitan folk songs. (The Roman songs reach back to the Middle Ages, while the Neapolitan songs are traditional but melancholy plaints of love.)

When the time comes to settle the bill, you'll find that La Cisterna is on the expensive side for Rome, with an average meal costing about 4000 lire ($6.60) per person. Yet it isn't too much to pay for the excellent food or the evening-long visit to the late seventeenth century. And it is a privilege to savor the atmosphere as well as the food which fed the spirit and body of the gallant Trilussa.

RESTAURANT—ROME

LE COQ D'OR

Via Flaminia Vecchia 493
Rome
Telephone: 393–247 (reservations necessary)

Open nightly 8 P.M.–1 A.M.
La cortesia: *Digestivo,* whiskey, or cognac
Expensive

The setting is a fifteenth-century villa overlooking the Tiber near the Ponte Milvio, the oldest bridge in Rome. Entering, you hear the soft chording of a guitar coming from the bar. Don't stop. Up the narrow, winding staircase, a dazzling fantasy-world comes to life—a large eight-sided room decorated with Renaissance art and a fresco that covers every inch of the domed ceiling. A crystal chandelier blazes with light. Giant logs crackle in the huge marble fireplace. A small bouquet of flowers reposes on every snowy tablecloth.

This is Le Coq d'Or.

Yet in summer, Le Coq d'Or is even more spectacular. For you eat outside, in a terraced garden, surrounded by exotic trees and beautiful sculptures, a setting for romance that can only be found in Rome.

With so splendid an atmosphere, can the food possibly live up to the ambience? It does.

Le Coq d'Or serves *soupe à l'oignon* as delicious as anything you get in Paris. Its *stracciatella* (eggs, flour, and Parmesan cheese flaked in broth like scrambled eggs) is an authentic Roman specialty. Its lobster bisque and turtle soup are excellent.

Of the main dishes, we particularly enjoyed the *steak tartare* (raw beef deliciously seasoned to one's own specifications), and the *paillard à la Richelieu* (thinly sliced veal, grilled and suitably flavored). On the left side of the menu, a box headed *"Specialità dello Chef"* lists the dishes of which His Majesty the Chef is especially proud.

The wine cellar at Le Coq d'Or is predictably large and familiar, but if you're ordering a well-seasoned meat you might consider *San Gimigneno,* a full-bodied local red, to accompany it.

Le Coq d'Or is expensive by Roman standards. Dinner for two—appetizer, main course, wine, dessert, and service—costs about $15.50. Afterwards, you'll be offered your *Discovery cortesia,* which may be whiskey, cognac, or the house *digestivo,* which bears the lilting name *misto amare de Valentino.* You may, if you wish, have it served at Le Coq d'Or nightclub. (See "Rome After Dark.")

English is spoken here, but it's hardly necessary. Le Coq d'Or's atmosphere and cuisine speak eloquently for themselves.

L'ESCARGOT

Via Appia Antica 46
Rome
Telephone: 513-6791 (reservations desirable)

Open for lunch and dinner (closed 3:30-6:30 P.M.) except Monday
La cortesia: Choice of *aperitivo* or *digestivo*
Moderately expensive

Some places are marked by history. L'Escargot is one of them.

Julius Caesar strode past its Appian Way site on his way home to Rome in triumph.

For hundreds of years, local peasants cavorted at a tavern in this very building.

The romance between Liz Taylor and Richard Burton began at L'Escargot.

But, while everyone has heard of L'Escargot and many say it's the best French restaurant in Rome, few have actually eaten there. The problem seems to be that L'Escargot's reputation is just *too* good. Roman aristocrats take their families there for dinner, foreign diplomats carry on informal negotiations there, European royalty dine there undetected—all in the understated atmosphere of a seventeenth-century country inn.

Yet there's nothing rustic about L'Escargot's food, a happy blending of the culinary backgrounds of Tuscany-born Signor Chabert and his signora Jeanne, who comes from a family of French restaurateurs. Their kitchen combines two of Europe's most notable cusines, and their wine cellar is a delight.

Begin with a half dozen *escargots de Bourgogne* (tender, meaty snails drenched in a delicate butter and garlic sauce). Then proceed to *steack au poivre flambé au Courvoisier* (sirloin steak seasoned with pepper and flamed in fine cognac), or *coeur de filet au madère* (filet mignon in madeira wine sauce). Don't miss the crisp, fresh *salade maison,* and be sure to try the delicious strawberry tart for dessert.

It is an honor to drink the wine at L'Escargot. Signor Chabert is a *tastevin* who travels widely throughout the French château country, and his wine cellar reflects it. If you're a *tastevin* yourself, ask to sample his Château Mouton Rothschild or Château Lafitte. On the other hand, he selects his local Italian wines with equal care, and they're much less expensive.

Dinner for two, including appetizer, main course, dessert, wine, and cover charge, comes only to about $12. And the service is excellent.

Giggi Fazi

RESTAURANT—ROME

Via Lucullo 22
Rome
Telephone: 464–045 or 478–928 (reservations recommended)

Open for lunch and dinner until late
La cortesia: Choice of *digestivo*
Moderate to expensive

Giggi Fazi is one of the funniest places in Rome. But you laugh *with* it, not *at* it. Matter of fact, "with it" are about the two most descriptive words for this *ristorante* near the Via Veneto. For this big, bright, cheerful place is where affluent Romans, leading politicians, and celebrities go to make the scene.

What is there to laugh at? All kinds of kooky things—toy stuffed animals and amusing little puppets scattered around, dried vegetables and huge hams dangling from the walls, a dripping faucet that's not connected to anything. Romans love this sort of thing.

The menu is decorated with a caricature of Giggi Fazi himself, a short bald man with heavy glasses and a perennial 5 o'clock shadow, and the specialties described inside are not just listed but *pictured* in a colorful, humorous way. That's fortunate, because the names are spelled out in a hip Roman dialect, sort of a pidgin Italian, so unless your *Italiano* is slangy and up-to-date, you'd be lost without the little drawings. But Giggi Fazi makes up for all this tomfoolery by very sensibly indicating the exact calorie count beside every dish—a big help if you've been eating your way through Europe and would like to cut down a bit.

Frankly, however, cutting down is a little difficult when you're confronted by one of Signor Fazi's glamorous *antipasti,* his luscious *lasagne al prosciutto (pasta* with ham), *penne con tonno* (wide noodles with tuna-fish sauce), *saltimbocca alla Romana* (veal and ham slices sautéed in butter and braised in white wine), or *cervelletto fritto dorato* (fried brains). And whatever else you order, be sure to have the *dolce St. Honoré* (cake), that delectable puff with the rum custard filling, for dessert.

Is it expensive? Well—sort of. Giggi Fazi is where Romans with money come to have a good time, while consuming positively enormous portions of food and wine. The cost of a meal is about $5 or $6 a person, a substantial amount by Roman standards

Yet it's worthwhile. For even if you don't always see the humor in what's going on, you'll get a kick out of watching the other guests—they think everything that happens here is a riot.

Ristorante Valle "La Biblioteca"

Largo Teatro Valle 9
Rome
Telephone: 651-292 (reservations please)

Open daily 7 P.M.–2 A.M. except August 10–30
La cortesia: Choice of *aperitivo* or *digestivo*
Moderate

When your Roman host says, "Let's meet at the library," chances are he's not talking about a book library at all. For "the library" is what Romans call one Ristorante Valle, where the wines are stocked library-style along the walls.

Valle was given its nickname as early as 1911, by students from the nearby University della Sapienza, who dropped into these cellars in the fifteenth-century *palazzo o*f Cardinal del Valle for a plate of *pasta* or a glass of *vino*. You'll see the logic behind it immediately. Hundreds, maybe thousands, of bottles are all neatly arranged in racks like shelves of books, occupying just about every surface of the *ristorante* except the ceiling and the stone arches. We doubt there is *any* wine, at least not any Italian wine, that couldn't be pulled from the shelves if you wanted it.

But if unusual décor and an extensive wine *lista* were all that Valle offered, it wouldn't have nearly the following that it has. Romans are as enthusiastic about food as about wine. Yet La Biblioteca's cellars are usually filled—with 380 people—every evening. For the food is excellent and the service is faultless.

Cannelloni deliziosi alla Valle, la nostra salsa per i gamberi cocktail (shrimp cocktail with a special sauce), *zuppa di cozze alla marinara* (mussel soup), and a delicious *filette di sogoliola* (filet of sole) are among the specialties. But the dishes we recall with greatest fondness are *ossobuco alla cremolata con risotto* (braised veal shanks with sweet marrow bone, resting on a bed of creamy rice) and *pollo alla Nerone* (broiled chicken flamed at the table).

Entertainment is supplied by a live orchestra, and on occasion you're treated to plaintive old Italian folk songs, as well. So all things considered, prices are moderate—about 3500 lire ($5.65) per person including cover and service.

"The library" has grown considerably since those pre-World War I days when it was the only cellar restaurant in Rome. But it is still operated by the founding family and—tribute to the quality of its cuisine—some of those long-ago students who first dubbed it *"La Biblioteca"* still turn up, in the company of their grandchildren.

ALL'ARCO DI S. CALISTO

Via Arco di S. Calisto 45, Trastevere
Rome
Telephone: 588–323 (reserve for evenings)

Open 1:00–4:00 P.M. and 7:30 P.M.–Midnight except Sunday
La cortesia: Choice of after-dinner drink
Moderate

Trastevere is deceiving. It is medieval *distretto* of peeling buildings and decaying streets, filled with quaint markets and tiny *trattorias*. Its residents are Roman artists and working people.

But side by side with this Trastevere is another Trastevere, where luxurious apartments hide behind façades deliberately kept in disrepair, and small galleries, antiquarian book and print shops, and splendid little *ristorantes* mix unobtrusively with the neighborhood markets. Its residents are Romans of affluence, young pace-setters, aristocracy. This is the Rome to which Arco di San Calisto belongs.

It is first and foremost a seafood restaurant, whose *lista* proclaims, with true Roman understatement, "soup and majestic fried fish." This is, of course, an English-language menu, which *proprietario* Signor Sabatini has thoughtfully put together. From his *lista,* our favorites were the mixed fried fish, which we cannot help but wish were still called *grigliato misto di pesce;* the grilled scampi with garlic butter, which ought still to be referred to as *scampi alla griglia;* and *triglia alla cartòccio,* which is half-translated as "red mullet in the *cartòccio*" *(cartòccio* means "paper bag," and this mullet is in fact grilled inside a greaseless bag and is delicious). Price of a complete meal—about 3000 lire per person ($4.85).

Arco di San Calisto is located near Trastevere's Piazza Santa Maria, in an area similar to Paris's Latin Quarter, except that here there are no automobiles to dispel the illusion of the Middle Ages. The *ristorante* itself is situated in a medieval house with low ceilings, and is decorated in simple rustic style. During the evenings, its clientele are entertained by singers and musicians.

Arco di San Calisto is an older brother to the nearby *ristorante* Sabatini, and *la cortesia* is the same—a choice of after-dinner drinks and, for the ladies, a ceramic wine decanter as a permanent reminder of a memorable meal in Rome. It occurs to us that with meat in one *ristorante* and fish at the other, you could start building a regular collection of decanters.

Ristorante "SABATINI IN TRASTEVERE"

Vicolo S. Maria in Trastevere 18
Rome
Telephone: 588-307 (reservations desirable in evenings)

Open 1:00–4:00 P.M. and 7:30 P.M.–Midnight except Tuesday
La cortesia: Choice of after-dinner drink
Moderate

Imagine dozens of hungry Romans happily having dinner in the street! Can't? Then you haven't been to Sabatini on a warm summer evening. The restaurant is so popular that, when the weather is right, it literally overflows its cellar of a 500-year-old house in medieval Trastevere. The intersections of Vicolo Santa Maria are then blocked off and Sabatini sets up tables along the entire street.

But no one minds being asked to dine at curbside. In fact, it's rather charming. And the food is so delicious that even the haughty Roman aristocracy pay strict attention to what's on their plates and palates rather than what's around them. (Of course, Trastevere is fascinating, but many of them live in the section and see it every day.)

Start at Sabatini with *tonnarelli alla ciociara* (noodles laced with mushrooms, beans, and ham), or *risotto alla pescatore* (shrimps, crayfish, squid, mussels, and clams on a bed of rice), then move on to a selection of *abbacchio allo spiedo* (milk-fed suckling lamb roasted on a spit in typically Roman fashion), *coda alla vaccinara* (braised oxtails with celery hearts), or *osso di prosciutto* (bone of ham garnished with beans.)

We would suggest that you choose your wine from among the many fine local varieties, perhaps a *Frascati* or a *Chianti*. After dinner, Signor Sabatini offers *Discovery* Card-holders a choice of after-dinner drink, and presents each lady in the party with an attractive wine decanter as a memento of their evening in his *ristorante*.

If you're in Rome when the weather is cold, don't forgo the pleasure of Sabatini in Trastevere because you don't want to eat outside. You won't have to. The cellar is simply but elegantly decorated, and you'll enjoy the small orchestra that plays typically Roman folk music. Prices, considering everything, are moderate—about 3000 lire ($4.85) a person.

Incidentally, if you're in the mood for seafood rather than meat or chicken, you might consider the *ristorante* Arco di San Calisto, one block away, which is under the same management but specializes in *pesce* and *frutti di mare*.

RESTAURANT—ROME

"*Cesarina*"

Via Sicilia 209
Rome
Telephone: 460–828 (reserve for evenings)

Open Noon–3 P.M. and 7 P.M.–Midnight except Fridays and
   August
La cortesia: After-dinner drink
Moderate

Signora Masi Cesarina has the look and warmth of an Italian Molly Goldberg. And once you see her, you know that behind her ample girth and impish smile lurk the talents of a marvelous cook. In Bologna, where the Signora ran a *ristorante* for many years before opening up near the Via Veneto in 1960, there is even a little toast to her prowess with *pasta* and *griglia:*

>
> *Cesarina, Cesarina,*
> *sei regina di cucina!*
> Cesarina, Cesarina,
> You are the queen of the kitchen!

The queen does not reign in a palace, however. Unlike many Roman restaurants, which are elegance personified, the *ristorante Cesarina* is plainer, like a classic *trattoria* from the Emilia region around Bologna. It consists of four rooms, all of them clean, airy, and decorated with mirrors. Not the least pretentious.

Nor is the food pretentious. Rather, it is simple and tasty, more like delicious home cooking, Bolognese style, than international *haute cuisine.*

Signora Cesarina herself manages the kitchen, personally selecting the all-important oils for cooking and seasoning, and buying the wines. Like her, they are from Emilia, for the Signora claims that one can do best when one is on familiar ground.

Our selections included *tortellini in brodo,* stuffed *pasta* rings in broth (not unlike Chinese *won ton* or Jewish *kreplach* soups), *misto Cesarina,* a house specialty which is really four different types of noodle mixed together, *bolliti misto carrello,* a hearty preparation consisting of seven different kinds of meat, and *cotoletta alla bolognese,* veal cutlet prepared with ham and prosciutto cheese.

Including cover charge, dessert, wine, and 12 percent *servizio,* the entire meal for two came to just around $9.

After dinner, Signora Cesarina will graciously offer *Discovery* Card-holders a *digestivo* of their choice, and suggests that during April or December it be the sweet, nut-flavored liqueur called *Nocino.*

RESTAURANT—ROME

La Villa dei Cesari

Via Ardeatina 164
Rome
Telephone: 513–6741 (reserve in summer)

Open daily, Noon till after Midnight
La cortesia: Any drink of your choice
Moderate to expensive

It often seems as if every place in Rome lays claim to *"la dolce vita,"* and hardly anything is written about the city without making at least a passing reference to this luxurious yet scandalous way of life. When La Villa dei Cesari boasts of *"la dolce vita,"* however, its credentials are more justified than most, for Anita Ekberg livened things up here long before she starred in the movie, and several important scenes from the film were actually shot in the restaurant.

La Villa dei Cesari has—you may recall this from the movie—a very unusual décor, which is that of Imperial Rome. Its food is cuisine to reckon with.

The restaurant is out near the ancient archeological digs, in the area of the old Roman road called the Via Appia Antica. Here, ever since the postwar recovery year of 1950, when Rome was first beginning to enjoy what later became known as "the soft life," Signor Libero Simmi has operated his own version of the Rome of the Caesars, complete with waiters dressed as Roman slaves.

We seriously doubt, however, that the average *civis Romanus* ever tasted food like Cesari's *fettucine alla Messalina* (thin ribbons of *pasta* laced with butter, eggs, Parmesan cheese, and ham), *maialino allo spiedo* (suckling pig roasted on a skewer), or *scaloppine di vitello alla Poppea* (veal sautéed in butter with beans and mushrooms). If you don't see them on the menu, ask for them. Signor Simmi runs a noteworthy kitchen, and these are his special dishes. A full meal costs 3000 to 3500 lire ($4.95 to $5.65) per person.

It's important to make reservations here, particularly during the summer months, when there's dancing. The rest of the year you'll be entertained by a highly talented guitarist with nostalgic Roman melodies.

La Villa dei Cesari is one of those places which you can enjoy on several levels—as entertainment, as fine Italian cooking, or simply because of its novel décor. The staff go out of their way to make sure you have a good time. They succeed admirably.

RESTAURANT—ROME

Helio Cabala

Via Spinabella
Marino di Roma
Telephone: 938-225

Open daily, Noon to Midnight
La cortesia: *Aperitivo* or *digestivo*
Moderately expensive

Pope Paul's summer retreat at Castel Gandolfo above you, Sophia Loren's country villa below you, a beautiful swimming pool beside you, and a delicious meal in front of you. That's what living is like at Helio Cabala, one of the most luxurious resort hotels in Italy. Our reason for mentioning it to you, however, is the restaurant, which is as far above the ordinary hotel restaurant as Castel Gandolfo is above Signora Ponti's villa.

Actually, there are three resturants here, as well as three bars, two swimming pools, and a nightclub, commanding a spectacular view of distant Rome. In fact, the entire complex is self-contained, with private cottages, narrow winding streets, boutiques, even a tiny church.

Our idea of the way to use Helio Cabala is to make an entire day of it, coming down for lunch or dinner and spending the afternoon swimming free of charge in one of the hotel's two pools (there are cabanas to change in at pool-side). The menu is 3200 lire ($5.16) per person *prèzzo fisso,* consisting of *antipasto; zuppa* (including minestrone and that Roman egg-drop soup called *stracciatella*) or *pasta;* a main course, which might typically be *saltimbocca alla Romana* (veal and ham slices sautéed in butter and braised in white wine) or *abbacchio scottadito* (lamb chop); dessert, which could be *torta gelata* (ice cream cake), ice cream, fresh fruit, or cheese; and coffee. Service is included, but wine is extra—800 lire ($1.30) a bottle.

Your *cortesia* is a choice of *aperitivo* or *digestivo,* and if it's the after-dinner drink that you want, you may have it served to you in the nightclub. Otherwise, Helio Cabala's nightclub has its own *cortesia* for you—the second drink on the house (provided you've purchased the first one).

To reach Helio Cabala, take the train marked "Castelli" from Rome's central railroad station to Marino, about 25 minutes (and 150 lire: 24¢) away. Phone from the Marino station, and the hotel will send a car down to get you.

Have a fine day!

Horti Galateæ

Via di Porta S. Sebastiano 5
Rome
Telephone: 779-933 or 753-330 (reserve during summer)

Open 11:30 A.M.–4:00 P.M. and 7:00 P.M.–1:00 A.M. daily except Tuesday
La cortesia: Choice of *aperitivo* or *digestivo*
Moderate

This is a summer place. The food is delicious all year round, and the atmosphere is always delightful, but summer touches Horti Galateae with magic. For the restaurant stands in the middle of its own lovely parkland, near the famous Baths of Caracalla, and in summer you eat outdoors under the trees. When *Carmen* is being performed over at the Baths, the stirring strains of the "Toreador Song" float across ancient Rome, and when *Aïda* is on, the trumpeting of elephants and the clank of armor can often be heard in the distance.

Even in Rome, there aren't many settings more romantic than this one.

But Horti Galateae has earned its reputation by serving the senses, not the soul. Its food is excellent. Start with *stracci alla Galatea* (cannelloni-shaped crepes stuffed with mozzarella cheese), *zite al prosciutto* (macaroni with butter, Parmesan cheese, and ham), or *tonnarelli alla ciociara (pasta* with mushrooms, ham, and beans). For your main dish, try the *scaloppine alla zingara* (veal with beans, mushrooms, and cheese), *filetto di tacchino al tegamino* (sliced breast of turkey sautéed in butter), or *mazzancolle alla pescatora* (scampi cooked on an open fire and served in the same plate they were cooked in). For dessert, order *torta al cioccolato* (chocolate cake) or fresh fruit.

Prices are generally moderate at Horti Galateae, but taking the magnificent setting and fine food into account, they're actually low. You'll pay about 2500 lire ($4) per person, including coffee and service. A bottle of good Italian wine raises the price another dollar or so.

Horti Galateae is an especially good bet for a late supper, after attending the opera at the Baths. Chances are that you'll even spot the tenor or *prima donna* of the evening eating at a nearby table.

La cortesia here is a choice of *aperitivo* or *digestivo,* but at certain times Signor Graziani, the manager, may offer you a special nut-flavored liquor in a small ceramic bottle. It's not always available, but when it is, you might want to try it.

RESTAURANT—ROME

Trattoria Archimede

Piazza dei Caprettari 78
Rome
Telephone: 561–616

Open Noon to Midnight except Monday
La cortesia: Drink before or after eating
Inexpensive

Archimede has several things going for it. It's well-located, just around the corner from the Panthéon. Its prices are low—you can get a full meal here for about 2200 lire ($3.55), or soup, main dish, and coffee for as little as 800 lire (about $1.30) plus tip. Its food is plain but good. And during the summer, its tables are set out on a large terrace and you eat in the Roman sunshine, (That's a rarity in this part of the city.)

Despite the humble prices and unassuming faré, the *casa* is a *castella* of courtesy and friendliness. *Proprietario* Umberto Vattani, who cooks and waits on table, and his daughter, cashier and general assistant to Papá, go out of their way to make you feel at home.

Most of the guests do feel at home, too, partly because they are neighborhood residents who know the Vattani family well. It was from one such habitué that we first learned of Archimede.

Our recommendations here would be *pollo alla Romana con peperoni* (chicken cooked with tomatoes and green peppers) for 650 lire ($1.05), or a delicious Roman specialty called *fritto di cervello animelle carciofi* (fried sweetbreads, brains, and artichokes) for 780 lire (about $1.25). Both are quite different from American food, but very tasty. The *saltimbocca alla Romana* (slices of veal and ham sautéed in butter and braised in white wine) is also good, and costs only 750 lire ($1.21).

Archimede has no wine cellar, so you must content yourself with the house *vino*. We found the local white wine to be especially dry and refreshing. It can hold its own with any but the most august products of the grape.

While the *trattoria* is without pretensions, it is clean, attractive, and well-run. The food is always well-prepared, the fruit is always fresh, and the service is always courteous. Moreover, the atmosphere is unfailingly cheerful, and when you eat on the terrace in warm weather, Archimede becomes positively romantic.

RESTAURANT—ROME

Re degli Amici

Via della Croce 33b
Rome
Telephone: 675–380

Open 9 A.M.–3 A.M. daily except Sunday
La cortesia: See below
Inexpensive

What do you do in a foreign city when you're out shopping at lunchtime and don't want to sacrifice two or three valuable hours lingering over a gourmet luncheon?

In Rome, if you're shopping on the Via Condotti, the answer is easy. Stop in Re degli Amici, on the nearby Via della Croce. True, it isn't a Roman temple of gastronomy, but it serves good substantial food at reasonable prices, and you'll be right in the neighborhood when the shops reopen in the afternoon.

Even in its simplicity, Re degli Amici has charm. The walls, for example, are decorated with scribbled sayings, signatures, and funny pictures, all left behind by customers. Lines like *Linda & Carlo* and *Giorgio and Sarah* are mute testimony to the large number of Romans who come here with their newfound American girl friends in the summertime.

Starter specialties are *cannelloni al re* (pipe-shaped *pasta* with mozzarella cheese), *rigatoni alla rigore* (noodles with ham, herbs, and tomatoes), and *spaghetti alla carbonara* (spaghetti laced with salt pork belly and eggs)—300 lire (48¢) an order. For your main dish, try *pollo con peperoni* (chicken with tomatoes and green peppers), *osso buco alla Romana* (braised ox shanks with marrow bone), *abbacchio arrosto* (roast lamb), or *gran medaglione reale* (steak with cheese, mushrooms, and ham, topped by an egg). Finish with a mild *caciotta bel paese* cheese or a sharp *gorgonzola groviera.* And wash everything down with the good house wine. The entire meal won't exceed 2000 lire per person—$3.25.

Your *cortesia,* if you're dining alone, will be a choice of *aperitivo, digestivo,* or coffee. *Proprietario* Antonio Latini will present two of you with half a liter of wine, and for four people together, the *cortesia* will be a full liter. In addition, you keep the pretty ceramic wine jug.

During the evening, Re degli Amici is a rendezvous for artists and journalists, and the combination of political issues and art trends sometimes generates heated discussions. But lunch is the best time to come, because of the convenient location and the good values.

RESTAURANT—ROME

Romolo

Via Porta Settimiana 8, Trastevere
Rome
Telephone: 588–284 (reservations helpful)

Open for lunch and dinner daily except Monday
La cortesia: Complimentary dessert after appetizer and main dish
Inexpensive

One is very close to the past in this charming and informal *osteria* in the picturesque Trastevere section. Not only do the houses on the narrow, winding streets date back to the Middle Ages, but some of the tales told in the district are fascinating.

We heard, for example, how during the sixteenth century the artist Raphael painted some frescoes on the walls of his mistress's apartment in the very building which Romolo now occupies. One day, so the story goes, Michaelangelo came up by chance when no one was home, saw the frescoes, and made his own changes in them. Raphael, overwhelmed at the maestro's interest, never completed the frescoes.

You won't be able to see them—if indeed they're still in the building—but Romolo is well worth visiting to feed the body if not the soul. Its typically Roman specialties are delicious.

Our choices for the appetizer were *spaghetti alla boscaiola* (with tuna-fish sauce) and *spaghetti alla carbonara* (with bacon and egg coating) at 340 lire each, about 55¢, followed by *saltimbocca alla Romana* (slices of veal topped with ham, seasoned and sautéed in butter, then braised with white wine) and *scallopine alla marsala* (veal prepared in white wine) at 800 lire each, about $1.30. For dessert, we ordered *gelato,* that splendid Roman ice cream, at 280 lire, about 45¢, a portion.

The entire meal for two, including wine (which cost about 66¢), coffee, and service, came to a ringing $7!

There are other typically Italian specialties on the menu that deserve special mention. If you visit Romolo in the spring, be sure to order *l'abbachio* (roast lamb) at its seasonal best. If you're a trifle adventurous, you might order the *trippa alla Romana* (tripe).

Romolo has been operated by the same family since 1870, and maintains a high standard of service, much appreciated by local Trastevere artists and among Romans who prefer well-prepared food to high-priced atmosphere. During warm weather, ask to be seated in the outdoor garden, which is roofed with grapevines. Informal and charming, Romolo is one of Rome's more enjoyable restaurants.

er "*faciolaro*"

PIZZERIA—ROME

Via dei Pastini 122–123
Rome
Telephone: 683–896

Open 11:30 A.M.–2:00 A.M. except Tuesday
La cortesia: Complimentary digestivo
Inexpensive

Here we go out on a limb—Er Faciolaro serves the best pizzas in Rome! That's what the Romans themselves say.

Why are they so special? Well, they're not thick and doughy, like so many of the pizzas served in America (and, unfortunately, in Rome itself), but light and flaky. And they come in seven different varieties—*Napoletana* (with anchovies, cheese, and tomatoes), *Margherita* (with tomatoes and cheese), *con salsiccie* (sausage), *con funghi* (mushrooms), *marinara* (with mussels), *mare* (seafood), and *capricciosa* (with mushrooms, bacon, egg, and olives).

These pizzas are sized individually, for one person rather than two or four, and cost between 200 lire (32¢) and 500 lire (80¢), inexpensive by American standards. Try to watch them being made because pizza-baking in Italy is considered a real art, and the two artists in the kitchen at Er Faciolaro fling the fresh dough back and forth with a spirit that verges on reckless abandon.

We were tipped off to Er Faciolaro by a newspaperman, who also touted us on *crostini*, an immensely popular Roman specialty, which is actually grilled Italian bread topped with cheese, ham, mushrooms, or paté. Very good—try it.

Besides the pizza and *crostini*, Er Faciolaro has another specialty—*fagioli*, which means "beans," and is a typical Roman dish. The word *faciolaro* actually translates as "bean-maker," so one would expect, correctly as it turns out, that all nine types served here are excellent. The beans, like the pizza, are tasty and inexpensive.

Er Faciolaro is, in fact, a very colorful place. A 40-year veteran of the Roman scene, it looks like an old stable, with herbs and dried foods hanging from the rafters. In the evenings, often as not, a folk singer will show up and entertain for handfuls of lire—not as part of an act but as part of a regular routine.

Here's a place to eat well, inexpensively, in the company of real Romans rather than tourists. Er Faciolaro is a lively and enjoyable place—it's full of beans!

"Il Barroccio"

Via dei Pastini 13–14
Rome
Telephone: 673-797

Open 11:30 A.M.–2:00 A.M. except Mondays
La cortesia: *Digestivo*
Inexpensive

It is astonishing how many different kinds of *pasta* there are in Rome. With few exceptions, they all taste pretty much alike, but they all look different. And with few exceptions, they all seem to be available at Il Barroccio.

As a starter dish, try the *bucatini alla matriciana* (a thin spaghetti with tomato, onion, and bacon sauce, served with sharp pecorino cheese). Or try as your main course *ruote al Barroccio,* a *pasta*-base meat dish *(ruote* are little pinwheels), which is one of the *casa*'s specialties. The *bollito misto alla Toscana,* a Piedmontese-descended mixture of boiled beef, tongue, chicken, sausage, and veal, served with a tart *salsa verde* (green sauce), is also delicious.

During the autumn months, Il Barroccio also lists fresh game and game birds among its specialties, and we are told—though we have no firsthand knowledge of the fact—that they, too, are extremely tasty.

If, on the other hand, you've decided that the time has come for something less exotic, stick to steaks—they're good here, and not expensive.

Whatever you order, you'll be pleasantly surprised by the bill, which rarely exceeds 4000 lire ($6.60) for two, and is often as low as 3200 lire ($5.15), including wine and 12 percent *servizio.*

Il Barrocchio is located in a Renaissance-era house next to the Panthéon, so if that's one of the sights on your morning agenda, you might keep the *ristorante* in mind. You'll find it a very cozy sort of place with the décor of a country inn, totally unpretentious and lacking in ceremony of any kind. Just plain good food, that's all. Il Barrocchio is practically unknown to tourists, but it's a big hangout for journalists from the *Stampa Estera* (press club)—which is important because newspapermen always know where to eat well for little money.

The manager, Signorina Agatha Guerri, offers as *la cortesia* an after-dinner drink such as anise-flavored *sambuca* or that powerful mountain brandy known as *grappa*. If neither appeals to you, she'll surely find a *digestivo* which does, because she and her *ristorante* regard a satisfied guest as the finest compliment in the world.

Ristorante "BUCA LAPI"

Via del Trebbio 1R
Florence
Telephone: 23–768 (reservations important)

Open daily except Monday, Noon–3 P.M. and 7–11:30 P.M.
La cortesia: Choice of *aperitivo*, cocktail, or house wine
Expensive

It takes a very confident *proprietario* to invite you into his kitchen before he shows you into his restaurant. But Signor Beppino Lapi does just that.

You enter the Ristorante Buca Lapi through the kitchen, where huge Florentine steaks are grilling over charcoal. What a marvelous aroma—a tantalizing suggestion of things to come! You proceed to the dining room which is papered with brilliantly colored travel posters from all over the world, sent here by its far-flung international clientele. You're seated, over a snowy white tablecloth, and now the pleasures begin.

First, dazzling *antipasto* from the cart, crisp fresh vegetables, sausages, paper-thin ham, olives, marinated mushrooms, hearts of artichoke. Then the house specialty, *bistecca alla Fiorentina*, served still sizzling from the grill, bubbling with its own juices and redolent with the flavor of charcoal. And big? Even if you're accustomed to king-size steaks, this one can easily be divided between two of you—in fact, the menu, with characteristic Florentine honesty, recommends just that. What to drink? What else but *Chianti Antinori*, that splendidly dry wine from Buca Lapi's own vineyard! And finally, a dessert of cheese—Bel Paese, Gorgonzola, or Parmigiano—and fruit.

If you don't feel like eating steak, the restaurant has a varied menu that includes such traditional dishes as *scampi* (giant shrimp), *osso buco alla Fiorentina* (veal attached to a shin bone that is filled with marrow), and *pollo alla Cacciatora* (chicken prepared with a tomato-scallion-mushroom-wine sauce).

The whole meal for two, complete with *pasta* and vegetable, won't run you more than $15 including tip.

Try to sit away from the music—the piano, violin, and singer are pleasant enough but a trifle too spirited at times, and sound better from afar.

Still, it's the food, not the entertainment that you come for. And Buca Lapi's lovely *bistecca* takes a back seat to no one's!

RESTAURANT—FLORENCE

Giannino in S. Lorenzo

Via Borgo S. Lorenzo 37-37R
Florence
Telephone: 272–206

Open daily 11 A.M.–11 P.M.
La cortesia: Complimentary *digestivo* in upstairs dining room
Moderate

In the likely event that you have never handled a medieval manuscript, laboriously hand-lettered and colored by monks in the *scriptorium,* we commend to you the menu at Giannino in S. Lorenzo. Obviously, it isn't a medieval manuscript, but it sure looks and feels like one.

We commend the menu for other reasons, too, one of them being its absolutely satisfying selection of Florentine specialties. The *minestrone di riso* was excellent—this hearty vegetable soup with rice added proved to be practically a meal in itself. The *scaloppa alla parmigiana,* famous as a dish in which veal is smothered by a heavy, sticky cheese, turned out here to be uncommonly light and flavorful—one tasted the veal rather than chewed relentlessly on the cheese. The *bistecca alla Fiorentina,* while not on the menu, turned up on request and was prepared exactly to our medium-rare specifications!

You should, when visiting Giannino in S. Lorenzo, take care to come *up*stairs to the airy, pleasant dining room, which is filled with delightful aromas and a colorful display of seasonal specialties of the *casa.* For the restaurant *down*stairs is a *rosticceria* with limited menu and limited service—a place for eating rather than dining. (Bear in mind, however, that it serves even in the mid-afternoon, and is a good place to get an excellent pizza if you've been out sightseeing and missed lunch.)

Signor Giovanni Mazzi, the host, belongs to the third generation of his family to operate the restaurant, which occupies what was once the *scuderia* (stables) of the four-centuries-old S. Lorenzo convent. He suggests—though the choice is yours—that your complimentary *digestivo* might be *grappa,* a powerful regional brandy which quickly separates the men from the boys. (Hemingway apparently liked it because, if you recall, his characters in *A Farewell to Arms* were forever swigging it.)

Prices at Giannino in S. Lorenzo are about 2500 lire ($4) per person at lunch and 3500 lire ($5.65) at dinner, during which a Florentine orchestra plays soft music-to-dine-by.

Giannino in S. Lorenzo is located right near the Duomo. But even if it were farther out, the combination of fine food and pleasant atmosphere would still make it well worth visiting.

RESTAURANT—FLORENCE

RISTORANTE PAOLI

Via Tavolini 12R
Florence
Telephone: 276–215 (reserve evenings and in summer)

Open Noon–3 P.M. and 7–10:30 P.M. except Tuesday
La cortesia: After-dinner drink
Moderate

Paoli bore the tragedy of the flood with the dignity of age. Established in 1827 in an authentic thirteenth-century *palazzo,* the *ristorante* caught the full force of Florence's disastrous 1966 flood, and is still in the process of recovering. Much of the original imitation thirteenth-century décor was swept away, and is now slowly, painstakingly, being re-imitated.

But if the décor is not yet entirely well, the quality of Paoli's food has fully recovered. Its Tuscan specialties would do honor to any connoisseur of fine Italian cooking.

Consider the *antipasto*—it includes *fagioli bianchi con caviale* (white beans with caviar), which are surely fit for a Medici. Consider the *cannelloni,* among the lightest and freshest we found in Italy. Consider the *scampi alla marinara,* spritely seasoned Adriatic shrimp brought in fresh daily. Consider the *bistecca alla Fiorentina,* a noble slab of steak, of which Paoli is rightfully proud. The selection of vegetables depends on the season, because the management wouldn't think of serving anything not absolutely fresh. For dessert, the *fedora,* a chocolate rum cake which is the house specialty, is unbeatable.

As we said, the food has fully recovered, and the vaulted *ristorante* with its wrought iron chandeliers and Florentine frescoes is rapidly resuming its pre-flood look. The original marble tables survived the waters and are back in place. The treasured guest book, which dates all the way back to opening day and contains some of the most famous signatures of the past century and a half, was saved from destruction and is there for you to see and sign. The service is as prompt and attentive as ever.

Prices at Paoli are quite reasonable. Two can enjoy a complete dinner—*antipasto, pasta,* main dish, dessert, wine, and service—for under $9.

Even in the 1970's Paoli will make you feel right at home in the thirteenth century.

Trattoria
"Sostanza"

Via del Porcellana 25R
Florence
Telephone: 272-691

Open Noon–2:30 P.M. and 7:30–10 P.M. except Sundays and holidays
La cortesia: Choice of *digestivo*
Inexpensive

Tucked away in the narrow, picturesque center of medieval Florence is a simple working-class *trattoria* called Sostanza. It is small, with space for only 40 people, who eat trencherman-sized portions of hearty peasant food at big marble tables seating six to ten people each. Since there are no private tables, total strangers eat together "Army-style."

What distinguishes Sostanza from countless other *trattorie* that line the streets of Florence—and many other Italian cities, for that matter—is the character of the customers and the quality of the food. For Sostanza, while it still attracts the streetcar conductors, also attracts the symphony conductor, and the president of a bank might well be seated beside a shop clerk or a street laborer. No one would care, for Sostanza is common ground. All are drawn here by the love of good food, well-prepared, well-presented, and then well polished off.

And what of the food? We'll not only recommend, but we'll also indicate prices, because the *lista* here is virtually unreadable. Start with the rich, hearty vegetable soup, *zuppa alla paesana,* for 250 lire (about 40¢). Then order *osso buco alla Fiorentina* (braised ox joint on a bed of rice) for 850 lire ($1.37), and be sure to eat the marrow. Or choose *stracotto alla casalinga con fagioli* (home-made pot roast with white beans) for 850 lire, or—if you're ready by now—*trippa alla Fiorentina* (braised tripe in tomato sauce), a Florentine specialty, for 500 lire (80¢). Finish off with *frutta* and *caffè*.

The entire meal shouldn't cost much over 2000 lire ($3.22). That includes the tip as well as a good Tuscan *Chianti* wine. But you can eat happily for much less, if you want to.

Sostanza has been serving like this ever since 1869, and Signor Giorgio Campolmi represents the third generation in his family to operate the *trattoria*. He knows everybody and everybody knows him. Moreover, the walls of his establishment are lined with cards and letters of praise sent by his guests, for his unassuming little *trattoria* with its plain and simple food and friendly manner has friends all over Italy.

Trattoria CAMMILLO

Borgo S. Jacopo 57R
Florence
Telephone: 272–427

Open Noon–3:00 P.M. and 6:30 P.M.–11:00 P.M.
La cortesia: Choice of *aperitivo* or *digestivo*
Moderate

It is interesting how, in Italy, the least pretentious restaurants are often the most sought after. Cammillo is a case in point. Cammillo, simply by serving honest food in a gracious manner, has found itself on the "favorite" list of such notables as the King and Queen of Denmark and Her Royal Highness Princess Margaret.

But Cammillo's prominence has not gone to the head of *proprietario* Bruno Masiero. Despite the acclaim of royalty and the favor of local Florentine nobility, he continues to treat each guest with the same courtesy and fine quality food that royalty and nobility enjoy.

So it is understandable that this *trattoria* in Oltrarno, the oldest section of Florence, should retain its simple rustic décor; that its wall decorations should be paintings from Signor Masiero's own collection and reflect his personal taste; that he should produce on his own land both the wine that guests drink and the oil that is used in the cooking; and that he should still tend to much of the cooking itself.

For simplicity is the keynote.

Yet there is in the food an element of the magnificent. The *taglierini al burro e trifola* (narrow strips of *pasta* laced with butter and truffles) is light and delectable. The *trippa alla Fiorentina* (braised tripe with tomato sauce) may even make a convert out of an American who raises a jaundiced eye whenever the word "tripe" is spoken. The *pètti di pollo alla Cammillo* (breast of chicken) is a marvel, and the *scaloppine Capriccio* (slices of veal served with truffles in a cream sauce) is worthy of a full page instead of half a sentence. Nor should a lover of seafood overlook the *scampi al curry e riso* or the *spaghetti alle vongole* (clam sauce)—they are small miracles.

Prices at Trattoria Cammillo are moderate—about 3000 lire ($4.85) per person for a meal that includes wine and 10 percent *servizio*.

Signor Masiero's establishment has moved a long way since he opened in 1946 with his entire family as his help. They, by now, have happily been able to return to the farm. But the signor remains, along with a staff of 14, to prepare and serve food fit for kings.

RESTAURANT—FLORENCE

OTELLO RISTORANTE

Via Orti Oricellari 28R
Florence
Telephone: 275–819 (reservations desirable)

Open daily Noon–3 P.M. and 7–11 P.M.
La cortesia: Choice of *digestivo*
Moderate

It's a peculiar thing about Italian restaurants. They're as likely to take the first name of the owner as the family name. Perhaps it's this homespun touch that builds public confidence; a man whose *ristorante* is called by his first name must still be humble enough to watch over it carefully.

Such, at any rate, is the case with Otello, whose *proprietario,* Signor Otello Giannoni, and his wife both guard the quality of the food every day. And the personal attention shows.

The reputation of the food attracts discriminating Florentines regularly. We were surprised, however, to find that not many travelers come in, especially since Otello is located right next to the railroad station. Their misfortune. They're missing some remarkable Tuscan specialties, including *penne trippa* (thick noodles generously interposed with tripe), *taglierini all'Otello* (noodles with truffles and peas), *rosto misto grillato* (a superbly seasoned mixed grill), and *filetto all'Alpino* (beef prepared in the northern Italian fashion—"like they do it on the mountains," Signor Giannoni told us).

After half a century as a restaurateur, he not only knows how to prepare and serve with singular subtlety but also how to please a guest's eye as well as his taste buds. Accordingly, the *ristorante* Otello presents itself as a rustic, typically Tuscan *osteria,* with wood paneling, natural vines and plants climbing a center post and decorating the walls, and a huge raised-hearth fireplace.

Although Otello is large, seating 200 guests in its three country-like rooms, it's a good idea to make advance reservations, especially on summer evenings. Come on down around 8 o'clock, enjoy a hearty meal and plenty of good red *Viticcio,* the house wine which appears to be related to *Chianti,* and get away for as little as 3000 lire (about $4.85) a person.

Otello may be only an unassuming restaurant down by the railroad station, but if you like good food in a charming atmosphere, its memory will linger.

«13 GOBBI»

Via del Porcellana 9R
Florence
Telephone: 298–769 (reservations advisable)

Open 11:30 A.M.–3:30 P.M. and 7–10:30 P.M. except Monday and August 1–15
La cortesia: Choice of *digestivo*
Inexpensive

The name is interesting. A bit of Florentine history. During medieval times, the almost-royal family of the Medici maintained its own court. And a court must have court singers, called *guillari* or *gòbbi*. At the court of the Medicis there were 13.

Trust Signor Rolando Lami, the *proprietario*, to know a thing like that. A highly cultivated man who speaks several languages and collects art, he is also something of an authority on the history and traditions of Florence. Such a combination naturally makes for interesting table-talk, especially when it can be coupled with praise for 13 Gòbbi's fine food.

We especially enjoyed the *risotto empolese con carciòfi* (rice with artichokes), *bistecca alla Fiorentina* (the famous Florentine steak which we often use as a quality control), and *bracioline di vitello chiantigiato e fagioli* (milk-fed veal cutlet with wine and kidney beans). We also noted a number of Hungarian specialties on the *lista,* and discovered that Signor Lami purchased his *ristorante* from a family of Hungarian restaurateurs in 1962. Rather than change the menu completely, and disappoint some of his guests, he simply learned how to cook Hungarian. Which gives you some idea of the type of attentive and concerned *proprietario* Signor Lami is!

Such a man, serving such food, has naturally built up quite a following among Florentine connoisseurs. And it *is* the food, not the atmosphere, they come to enjoy. For 13 Gòbbi is certainly not overpoweringly traditional in appearance. Rather, it's a bright, airy, thoroughly modern establishment that has almost the appearance of an American cocktail lounge. (Indeed, Signor Lami often refers to it as his *birreria*, his "beer garden.")

Prices at the "beer garden" are on the modest side—an entire meal shouldn't cost much more than 2200 lire (about $3.55) per person. But it's a good meal, a fine meal, prepared by a splendid young chef and served with care and dignity by a second-generation restaurateur with over half a century of experience in his field.

Though 13 Gòbbi is tucked away on a small street and is difficult to find, an effort should be made.

Restaurant da Piero

Via Lamberti 5R
Florence
Telephone: 23–381

Open Noon to Midnight, daily except Monday
La cortesia: Complimentary *digestivo* after three-course meal
Inexpensive

Piero is simplicity itself—just tables and chairs in an old house on a side street about midway between the Piazza della Signoria and Piazza della Repubblica. All that it has going for it are honest food, deliciously prepared, and service that attends every guest as if he were the first. Of décor, there is none—except fresh flowers constantly on the tables.

But unless you're an unrelenting seeker after atmosphere, Piero will please you immensely. Its very simplicity is elegant. Through the furniture is plain and the walls are sterile, the place is cozy and the staff, led by Signor Piero Merciai, really *care*. We mention all this by way of explaining that, although the outside world has never heard of Piero, its 180 places are constantly filled with Florentines—and not just any Florentines: Florentine gourmets who are finicky about cooking.

Assuming that you're finicky, too—and why not? it's what makes for good eating!—lead off with *risotto salsa funghi* (rice in mushroom sauce). Then turn to any of several delicious main dishes—including *pètto di cappone Merciai con trifola* (breast of capon), *scallopine alla San Marco,* or *còstola di vitello alla zingara* (lamb chop prepared, says Signor Merciai, "in the Gypsy way"). All arrive at your table with the steam still rising and the flavor poised to be released on your palate. Wine selection, which poses a problem in many more pretentious restaurants, creates no difficulty here—just drink the local red Tuscany wine. Maybe it isn't as distinguished as some of the vintages from over the border in France, or even some of the bottled-for-export Italian varieties, but it's dry and honest and entirely flavorful.

Because you pay only for food and wine, not overhead, Piero's prices are relatively low—a complete three-course meal with wine and service costs between 2000 and 2500 lire a person ($3.35–$4). There are many establishments, even in Florence, where you'd pay a great deal more money for a great deal less quality.

Where to Buy Clothes: Shopping Discoveries

Where to Buy Clothing and Accessories: Shopping Discoveries

During the fall, Florentines motor down to Rome to purchase high-fashion apparel. Comes the winter, and Romans drive up to Florence to do their Christmas shopping.

No matter what season of the year you come, shopping in these two cities can be a marvelous adventure accompanied by a constant sense of discovery.

Rome is fast becoming an international leader in high fashion for both men and women. Many of the outfits and accessories featured on the pages of leading fashion magazines around the world now come from Rome.

So shopping there is no longer cheap. The prices can run well up into the range of the better New York shops. But the merchandise is beautiful, imaginative, and elegant, and the workmanship is unexcelled.

Indeed the quality and variety of merchandise appears better today than it was just a few years ago. Thanks to Italy's "Economic Miracle," more Italians have more money to spend than at any time in history, and they are demanding more and better goods for themselves.

Boutiques for men and women are opening in Rome by the dozens. A few are simply expensive with not much else to commend them. But many carry tasteful, imaginative merchandise of every kind and description.

For women you'll find beaded boots, exotic pajamas, bejeweled belts, and colorful sportswear, as well as beautiful lingerie, knit dresses, and stylish coats and suits.

For men you'll come upon safari suits, maxi coats, leather jackets, silk ties, cashmere sweaters, and a large selection of elegantly tailored suits and coats.

Perhaps the single biggest change in women's clothing in recent years is the development of ready-to-wear. Roman women are discovering what Americans have known for years, that ready-to-wear apparel, tastefully done, can be just as interesting and less expensive than custom tailoring.

But Italian ready-to-wear is special. It has not reached the stage of mass production that is found in other countries. Italian products are well-tailored and detailed, much of the sewing is still done by hand, and the fabrics are of superior quality.

In men's fashions, the tradition of custom tailoring remains strong, although ready-to-wear is beginning to make inroads here as well. If you're interested in having a man's suit custom-tailored, Rome is an excellent place for it. (Many of the better tailors in the United States and Canada, today, came originally from Italy.)

Several men's-wear designers and tailors are now producing their own line of ready-to-wear clothing, at prices below their custom-made products.

Children's ready-made clothing is found in abundance in Rome. It is certainly among the most beautiful children's merchandise to be found anywhere, and the detailing and design are delightful. The prices are on the high side.

Rome is an easy town for shoppers because there is a specific shopping district. At one time, Via Condotti used to be *the* street for fashionable shopping. It still is fashionable, but the shops have spread out into nearby streets as well.

The major shopping streets for clothing start in the Piazza Di Spagna, and end with the Via del Corso. It's a smaller area, so a walking tour is easy. Begin with the Piazza and weave down through the Via delle Carrozze, the Via Condotti, Via Borgognona, Via Frattina, and Via della Vite. And don't forget the Piazza and the Corso themselves. Another day, you might want to start at the Piazza again, and head in the other direction up to Via Sistina.

Almost all our Shopping Discoveries are on or near these few streets. The remainder are only a short walk or taxi ride away.

The old rule that you bargain on prices in Rome no longer applies. While there are still some exceptions, prices in the better fashion shops are rapidly becoming as fixed as in New York or London.

Despite the changes, one characteristic of shopping remains constant—the hours during which the shops are open for business. The Romans still close for a long lunch period in the middle of the day, so the hours of business are complicated.

> Winter hours (from October 15 to the end of March) are from 9 A.M. to 1 P.M. and again from 3:30 P.M. to 7:30 P.M.
>
> Summer hours (from April 1 to October 15) are from 9 A.M. to 1 P.M. and again from 4:00 P.M. to 8 P.M.

To further confuse matters, some shops close on a particular weekday morning. And a few, very few, establishments have adopted the non-Roman custom of staying open during lunch and closing early. Unless otherwise noted, the hours listed above apply to the shops on the following pages.

Now to Florence:

Florence is undoubtedly one of the best cities in the world for shopping. In clothing and accessories, the key attraction is leather, in every shape and form. This is the city in which you buy leather coats, leather dresses, leather pants, leather gloves, and leather bags. The quality is excellent and the prices are unbeatable.

Every year, buyers from department stores in the United States, Canada, and the rest of Western Europe, all converge on Florence. But fortunately, success has not ruined Florentine workmanship. The standards of quality are being maintained and the sense of design has improved.

Florentine shoes are renowned for their styling and workmanship, and you'll find several fine shoe salons that display the local wares. (Italian shoes are built to the scale of Italian feet which, somehow, aren't the same as North American feet. Try the shoes, by all means, but be sure they're comfortable before you buy.)

Bags, coats and accessories, of course, should prove no problem. The prices on these items are considerably higher than they were a few years ago, but they're still a good buy by American standards.

Ready-to-wear clothing is beginning to make an impact in Florence, also. The best buys for women are in Italian knitwear. The noted, long-established Florentine clothiers—for both men and women—have recently added ready-to-wear merchandise that's shown alongside their traditional tailoring materials. French imports also are popular and good buys. Embroidered lingerie is another Florentine specialty.

The street pattern in Florence is irregular and confusing. But it's a small town, so the best way to get around is on foot. The trick to shopping is to locate the four major shopping streets and mark them off on a map.

Start with the Via Tornabuoni, the most elegant street in Florence. Then locate Via Calziuoli which runs from the Piazza Duomo to the Piazza della Signoria.

For the third street, locate the Via Roma (which runs parallel to Via Tornabuoni and Via Calziuoli). Via Roma changes its name along the way to Calimala and Por. S. Maria—but continue it to the famed Ponte Vecchio bridge.

Cross the bridge and you come to Via Guicciardini on the other side of the Arno. This is the fourth major street.

You might also want to note the Via Strozzi, which runs perpendicular to and connects with Via Tornabuoni, Via Calziuoli, and Via Roma.

Crossing from one of these streets to another will take you past numerous interesting side streets. Stop off by all means, but keep your eyes on these main arteries and you won't get lost.

You'll notice, on your walks, such well-known names as Gucci for leather goods, Pucci for fashions, and Buccellati for jewels. We have not included these places in our book, simply because they are not "discoveries." These firms have had international reputations for many years, and have their own shops in the United States. Nevertheless, they are worth a visit.

Florentine shopping hours are similar to but not identical to those in Rome:

Winter hours are 9 A.M. to 1 P.M. and again from 3:30 P.M. to 7:30 P.M.

Summer hours are 9 AM. to 1 P.M. and again from 3:30 P.M. to 8:00 P.M.

One thing should be mentioned: the prices quoted at individual shops are the list prices in the shops *before* the *Discovery* discount is applied.

Also, the rating of the shops in terms of price category is based on local Roman or Florentine standards. What's expensive to a Roman or Florentine may or may not be expensive to you.

BEATRICE
Via F. Crispi 80
Rome
Telephone: 487-806

Open daily except Sunday
10% discount
Medium high

Beatrice is a treat.

It's the kind of boutique in which you want to try on almost everything, because you're positive the styles were made just for you. That's the secret of Signora Beatrice's success—she knows how to do classic and high-styling with a flair that will suit women of varying dispositions and age. And at prices that make her outfits among the best buys in Rome.

One thing, though—the designs are for smaller, youngish-looking women. The sizes run in what is the equivalent of 8 to 14 American, with just a few size 16's.

The boutique is one of the few Roman shops that's chock full of ready-to-wear merchandise. That's because the firm does a large volume of business, selling to other shops throughout Italy as well as to better shops abroad. The boutique reflects the best of the firm's designs.

Signora Beatrice herself is a bright bundle of energy who looks great in her own clothes. She started in the fashion business 20 years ago by working for other fashion houses. During that time, she began designing dresses and making collections for her friends. The success of this sideline prompted her to open her own fashion house together with a business partner, Signor Guido Bianchi. Their establishment, opened in 1953, was successful almost immediately. When ready-to-wear fashions came to Italy, the Signora was ready to capitalize on the trend.

Beatrice prepares new collections twice a year, and her showings always draw overflow crowds.

She designs her own beautiful fabrics, and sometimes has French fabrics copied in Italy. That's one factor that keeps the prices below what you'd expect.

Some sample prices: $45 for a winter dress; $96 to $126 for a dress with jacket; $110 for a coat; $193 for a coat and dress outfit of the finest fabric; $89 for a suit; $78 for a woolen and silk pants suit; $29 for a summer dress.

Asked what accounts for her phenomenal success, Beatrice explains, "My line is rather classic, but the details and handwork make it something special. It make things that I personally like and the quality must be first-rate. It's elegant fashion with a touch of *haute couture*, but at a more favorable price."

DESIGNER ORIGINALS—ROME

Via de Ripetta 22
Rome
Telephone: 679-0941

Open daily except Saturday and Sunday, 10:00 A.M.–6:00 P.M.
10% discount on ready-to-wear only
Medium high

If you've seen magazine articles about the rise of Italian fashions, chances are you've admired the works of Lydia de Roma. She is a recent winner of the Nieman-Marcus award for top designers, and her unusual styles are worn by well-dressed women around the world.

Lydia combined Italian hand-embroidery with sophisticated design to pioneer a new look in international fashion.

"I thought it was a waste to save all that beautiful embroidery for linens and towels. Women's clothing should be gay and fun and beautifully made."

After World War II, when most Italian women were still garbed in basic black, Lydia grouped together Rome's handicraft workers and went into business. She convinced her then-clientele that even an old sheet, by being embroidered, could be transformed into a beautiful summer dress; that a gingham tablecloth could be used for a blouse; that peasant-type embroidery and beautiful silk could be compatibly worked together to make a stunning outfit. Lydia anticipated, by many years, the patchwork look in clothing that's so fashionable now.

Today the firm employs 180 workers, but the garments are all still worked by hand. The specialties are summer and cruise wear, but even the sweaters that the boutique carries for winter are hand-loomed.

The boutique is located in a sixteenth-century palace near the Piazza del Populo. To find it, enter the building's courtyard and look for the sign that says Studio Room. (Don't confuse it with the firm's workshops located nearby.)

If you are fortunate enough to find one of the boutique samples in your size, the *Discovery* discount applies. Otherwise any garment can be made to order and shipped to you at home (no discount on special orders).

Summer dresses are $30 and up depending on the amount of hand embroidery and the material used. An embroidered coat with dress to match can run much higher. Sportswear such as a slack and sweater set run about $50. Wool dresses sell for $60 to $100.

KNITWEAR BOUTIQUE—ROME

L. Spagnol

Via delle Carrozze 69
Rome
Telephone: 683–569

Open daily except Sunday
10% discount
Medium

To our mind, this shop sells some of the best medium-priced Italian knitwear.

Spagnol is tucked away on a small street just off the Piazza Di Spagna. Its clientele are mostly Italians who like the combination of quality and price that you get here. The shop is new to Rome, but it is the retail outlet for a well-known Italian knitwear factory—L. Spagnol—which has been exporting its goods abroad for many years. Now these fine-fashioned knits are available in Rome.

There is a large supply of stock on hand—including coats, dresses, and pants. And if you see something you like that's not available in your size, it can be made for you within a matter of days.

In addition to its own line, the shop carries a good selection of French imports, as well as some of the more outstanding and interesting merchandise of other Italian manufacturers. The styling runs from youthful to fashionable. The clothes have flair without being flashy.

Some sample prices: Summer knit dresses of cotton and Banlon sell for about $30. A linen dress sells for just over $30. The costliest summer item is a beautiful printed silk jersey dress that is made up in a variety of patterns and styles and sells for $80.

Dresses in wool knit for fall, winter, and spring range in price from $25 to $80, with a good selection all along the line. Wool coats run up to $250 for one with fur trim. (It should be noted, however, that Italian winter coats are generally lighter in weight than those sold in the cold weather regions of the United States and Canada.)

One of the more interesting outfits is a knit, double-faced coat that can be worn on either side; it sells for $120. An unlined knit coat sells for half that price. Knit pants go for $24 and a pants outfit for $73.

Signora Bisotti, the shop's manager, is now taking English lessons. The rest of the staff is multilingual, and since all the merchandise is displayed with fixed prices attached, you should encounter no problems in making a selection.

SPECIALTY BOUTIQUE—ROME

MIRANDA

Via delle Carrozze 22B
Rome
Telephone: 682-793

Open daily except Sunday
10% discount
Medium

Miranda is one of those unusual little shops that is tucked away on the side streets of Rome, just a few short blocks from the center of the shopping district.

Miranda's specialty is mohair—a soft, hand-loomed fabric that's woven into solids, plaids, tweeds, into caftans, ponchos, triangles, scarves, coats, suits, dresses, and long skirts.

The shop has a loom on which you can watch the fabrics being woven. And there are other looms at the factory which services this establishment.

The results are not at all "craftsy"-looking. Instead the ready-to-wear items are fashionable and tasteful. The long skirts (about $36) are perfect for after-ski wear. The coats (about $75) are warm and beautifully styled. The ponchos and long lean scarves with matching berets are the rage now for fashionable young Romans, yet prices are modest. The mohair items are available all year around. If you come in summer you'll also find hand-woven linen and cotton items.

In addition to the ready-to-wear, you can have a special order ready within 5 to 8 days. Since Miranda does much exporting, they're used to shipping goods.

We asked Signora Miranda Riccetti, the owner, how she became involved with hand-looming. Her grandmother, she told us, was an Indian princess who lived in England. It was from her that Signora Miranda acquired her interest in handsome fabric. She began many years ago with one loom at home, but the hobby soon became a business, and Signora Miranda has been selling to better shops around the world for 18 years. Her clientele in Rome are mostly Italians and a few resident Americans.

FASHION JEWELRY BOUTIQUE—ROME

LUCIANA

Via della Vite 93
Rome
Telephone: 684–626

Open daily except Sunday
10% discount
Medium high

Luciana's jewels are not for everybody.

But for the woman who is a faithful reader of *Vogue* and *Harper's Bazaar*, and a believer in high fashion, a visit to this boutique is in the nature of a pilgrimage.

Luciana of Rome is actually the Baroness de Reutern, an amazingly creative woman whose designs are revolutionizing the world of what used to be called "costume" jewelry. "Fashion" jewelry is a better word for it, for the pieces she creates grace the covers and pages of better fashion magazines almost every month. Luciana's clip book about her work runs into the hundreds of pages.

That high-fashion model with the sloe eyes and the broad Egyptian-like collar necklace is wearing a Luciana work. Those combination ring-bracelets fashioned with mirrors, those strange-looking sun patterns on rings and necklaces, those important pieces with an antique ruggedness to them—all are Luciana's works.

Many of her recent pieces were inspired by themes of the Etruscans, that high civilization which preceded the Roman in Italy. All the jewelry is hand-hammered, and plated in 24K gold with a satin finish.

However, you needn't be a model to carry off these pieces. Many of the designs are simple and wearable. Yet they can transform an ordinary black dress into something very special.

"I believe that good jewelry must be becoming to a woman and to her clothes," explains Luciana. "It should not be simply the placing of wealth upon a person."

The prices—surprisingly modest for the skill that goes into each piece. Necklaces average $20 and may go up to $42 for the most elaborate. Earrings sell for $10 to $21. Rings are $8 and up.

This famous designer sells to boutiques and fine shops around the world. Here in Rome, you can buy her works directly at the source.

FASHION JEWELRY BOUTIQUE—ROME

"Nucci"

Via Gregoriana 55A
Rome
Telephone: 672–273

Open daily except Sunday
10% discount
Medium

Signora Nucci is another of those remarkable talents which seem to thrive in Rome by turning a small hobby into a successful business. Even as the business grows, the creativity and quality workmanship which prompted its initial success continue to remain strong.

Nucci's forté is fashion jewelry made of beads. Sounds simple, but somehow the tiny beads, with the help of several nimble-fingered assistants, are transformed into stunning pearl belts, collar necklaces, and beaded halters—all of which are very much in vogue just now.

You'll see Signora Nucci's jewels being worn by fashion models and movie people. The month we visited her shop, two of her halter necklaces were gracing film stars photographed for the cover of a national magazine. Signora Nucci sells to boutiques, to fashionable Romans, and to couturier houses which then incorporate her work into their own line of clothes.

The prices are surprisingly modest for the workmanship that goes into them. We saw a beautiful silver-colored belt for $13. Earrings for winter wear, which have more expensive beads, are priced between $8 and $19. Colorful summer earrings cost between $4 and $6 the pair. Elaborate collar necklaces sell for between $16 and $40, and gaily beaded bags go for $29.

The Signora loves to show her wares to appreciative customers, and with her petite figure and looks, she is her own best model. The shop, which is also the workshop, appears small, but there are all sorts of exciting objects tucked away in nooks and drawers.

A Nucci accessory may not be necessary to give a new look to a favored old dress—but it helps!

tomassini

Via Sistina 119
Rome
Telephone: 461-909

Open daily except Sunday
10% discount on ready-to-wear merchandise
Expensive

This is the shop for men who want to buy something special for their wives, and for women who *are* something special. Tomassini sells the kind of lingerie women dream about—delicate, beautifully made, hand-finished, and sumptuous.

Signora Luisa Romagnoli, the proprietress, opened this business over 20 years ago. She designs all the garments herself and oversees their preparation. Over the years she has built up a faithful following.

"I aim for a stylish and elegant look—something different, yet lasting," she explains. "My customers include well-to-do Romans and Italians from all over the country, as well as many foreigners. Mothers whom I've outfitted come and ask me to do trousseaus for their daughters."

Hand embroidery, extensive pleating, beautiful laces and trims are marks of the Signora's work. The materials used are silk, cotton, nylon, and soft, soft wool, always of the best quality.

Pick up a delicate lace slip and you're likely to find hand-embroidered flowers worked into the lace. That soft-looking peignoir is all hand-crocheted. Those lace handkerchiefs are almost too precious to use, and the initialing on them reflects hours of hand-work.

Naturally, with all that going for it, the prices are bound to be somewhat high, at least by Roman standards. Slips start at $6.80 and a very fine detailed slip goes for $15 or $20. Long robes start at $22. A peignoir and nightgown fit for a trousseau may be had for $64. The embroidered and lace handkerchiefs range from $3 to $10 each.

In addition to the large amount of ready-to-wear, Tomassini will make lingerie to order.

All in all, this is unquestionably one of the finest lingerie shops in Rome.

Dell'Ariccia

Piazza Di Spagna 7
Rome
Telephone: 672–198

Open daily except Sunday
10% discount
Medium to high

Dell'Ariccia has been a fixture on the Piazza Di Spagna ever since 1945. More to the point, its wares seem to be just about twelve issues ahead of American fashion magazines. Which means that the ladies' bags and accessories displayed here are likely to be very much in style at home next year.

That accounts for the fact that a number of American boutique-owners were doing their own shopping here on the morning we arrived. They were getting a peek at next year's merchandise in their own shops! And they were ordering.

One of the reasons Dell'Ariccia is so popular—and not only with visitors—is its policy of gathering a wide selection of bags made by manufacturers throughout Italy. Because of this large inventory, prices and styles range widely.

From the standpoint of style, for instance, bags are classic as well as very contemporary (we particularly liked those with a crushed patent look and snake-imprinted leather). We found 30 different styles of brown bags, even more styles in black bags! From the price point of view, we saw a leather clutch bag for $10, dozens of interesting leather bags for about $30, and even a few alligator bags in the $300 range.

Luggage (about $80 for a large suitcase), gift items, and signature scarves make up the balance of Dell'Ariccia's inventory.

Despite the steady stream of English-speaking buyers, most of the clientele is Roman. Yet enough overseas boutique-owners come regularly, and enough American travelers come during the summer months, to have forced charming Signora Tirassa to acquire a bit of English. She can, therefore, explain to you the major merits of her merchandise. Not that it matters much. Dell'Ariccia's bags speak for themselves—in the international language of fine fashion.

Raphael's

Via della Vite 45
Rome
Telephone: 679-1912

Open daily except Sunday
15% discount
Inexpensive to medium

In a city that specializes in high-priced leather goods, Raphael's wares are aimed at the young and budget-minded. The quality is fine but the prices are low. The styles are young and swinging.

A smaller leather clutch bag costs from $5 to $13. Leather bags sell from $13 to $26, and many come in casual shoulder-strap style. Wallets are from $4 to $8, and other leather gifts items start at $4.80.

If you're in need of an extra suitcase, as we were, luggage is a good buy here. Simulated leather suitcases in air weight run from $10 for a small bag to $21 for a large one; leather luggage runs from $23 to $48.

Raphael's is run by Signora Rossana Fiore and Signor Rossell, two earnest young people who learned their business by actually working for years in the leather trade. They know their merchandise, and they know where to find the best quality for the money.

Also ask to see the shop's selection of fun furs and leather coats, which are tucked away on the side. We especially liked a leather coat with fox trim that sold for $240, and some rabbit-fur coats that sold for between $97 and $113. Suède jackets for men are priced from $45 to $81; for women they are $56.

The shop opened its doors in 1969 and is located in the central shopping area. Judging by the satisfaction of its customers, it's likely to be around for a long time.

Aldo Di Cori
Piazza Di Spagna 53
Rome
Telephone: 684-439

Open daily except Sunday
10% discount
Medium

Italy is so well known for leather gloves that many Americans, when they come here, go a little glove-happy, buying dozens of pairs at a time. And why not? Prices are very reasonable. After all, in Italy, leather gloves are the only type deemed appropriate for a lady's wardrobe, and cost relatively little.

Di Cori does its part to keep the prices modest, which perhaps accounts for its growth—manufacturing facilities, four shops, and an export business, as well.

Here at the Piazza Di Spagna shop, the selection is unusually large, with gloves for women coming in all lengths, all colors, and dozens of patterns. Materials are either kid or antelope.

Men's gloves come in styles made for driving, for dress purposes, or simply for warmth.

Prices? Well, for women they start about $2.25 and rarely go over $7.25. For men, $3.10 to $4. For children, $2. (Tip from Signor Di Cori: if you wish to buy children's gloves, bring along a hand-outline, and the shop will match it.)

Di Cori has been in business since 1932, and like many Roman enterprises is family-run. The elder Signor Di Cori founded the firm, and now his three sons operate it together. Since they make all their own gloves in their own factory, they can afford to keep prices in the medium range—important not only to Romans but to glove-shopping visitors.

Other Di Cori locations: Via del Tritone 52, Via Nazionale 183, and Via Gioberti 69.

LEATHER SPECIALIST—ROME

GINO COSTA saddler

Via Frattina 113
Rome
Telephone: 679–6001

Open daily except Sunday
10% discount
Medium

The heady aroma of fine leather pervades the air in this authentic Roman saddler's shop. A saddler—that's a specialist in leather, a man who takes the raw material and transforms it into something else. It does not mean (and we might as well point it out at the start) a man who necessarily makes saddles. Yet we have no doubt that Gino Costa could, if he chose, do very well outfitting the cavalry in all those Italian-made western movies, for he's one of the very best saddlers in Rome.

The leather coats, shoes, belts, and women's wear fashioned by Gino Costa reflect an individuality in design and workmanship that's a pleasure to touch and wear. Romans think so, too. They come here from all walks of Roman life in order to find something distinctive to wear. And they find it.

In 1967, Gino Costa won the Gold Medal awarded for leather style and workmanship in Florence, a city where the competition in leatherwork is especially keen. In 1968, he won an international prize for high fashion in Turin, Italy. But his proudest award, he says—an award that he has been winning regularly ever since opening his shop in 1955—is the acclaim of leather-loving Romans.

The shop here on Via Frattina looks like a workroom, but is actually a small and busy boutique with a variety of merchandise on display for both men and women. The items already in the shop may be purchased, of course, but they also serve as samples of what can be made up for you on special order.

Some representative prices: coats from $110 to $150, shoes from $15 to $25, belts from $8 to $15, and luggage from $80 to $130.

If you like the look and feel of fine leather, you'll love the products of Gino Costa—saddler extraordinary.

PIATTELLI

Via del Corso 184—men's made-to-measure
Via Convertite 19—men's ready-to-wear
Via Condotti 20A—women's wear
Rome
Telephone: 672-450

Open daily except Sunday
10% discount on custom tailoring
5% on ready-to-wear
Expensive

If you've ever been tempted to order tailor-made clothes, Piattelli may well make that temptation irresistible.

For here at the luxurious Via del Corso showroom, you'll be offered some of the most attractive material and tailoring for men in Rome. Signor Piattelli is a renowned designer whose styles range from contemporary to classical.

Ideas, new colors, and even fabrics are originated by this inventive firm. Here, you'll see three-piece suits made not with a vest, but with trousers, jacket, and shirt that all go together. You'll see rain outfits that include waterproof trousers, tunic, and a double-breasted raincoat. And in a more traditional vein, you'll find beautifully tailored blazers.

Be prepared to spend $245 for a suit, close to $300 for a coat, $30 for a shirt, and $160 for a blazer. It's costly, but it's men's tailoring on a grand scale.

(To find the showroom, enter the building and go up the stairs, through a long lobby which is often filled with art, till you get to the Piattelli receptionist.)

For the same kind of tailoring but at lower prices, head for Via Convertite 19. That shop carries the designer's line of men's ready-to-wear—suits $80 to $115, shirts $16 to $18, ties $7 to $9, sweaters $30, and coats $70 to $115.

If your wife is longing for a Piattelli outfit of her own, that can be arranged as well. Simply head for the third shop on the Via Condotti. It specializes in women's wear, both custom and ready-made. We found the tweeds here especially appealing and thought that they were made up into some of the most attractive sports outfits around Rome.

The cool weather ready-to-wear includes three-quarter-length coats ($150) designed to go with pants ($53), knit jacket and matching pants ($90), suits ($230), and coats ($160).

The summer ready-to-wear features bikinis ($14), beach jackets ($32), linen slacks ($20 to $23), and silk slacks ($33). Custom tailoring runs slightly higher.

SHOES FOR MEN AND WOMEN—ROME

Sanna

Via del Corso 483–484
Rome
Telephone: 672–746

Open daily except Sunday
10% discount
Expensive

Sanna is one of those rare workshops which still can be found in Rome. Its product is shoes, but these are no ordinary shoes; every pair is handmade and of the finest quality. The designs are the shop's own and are very fashionable. But, if you prefer, Sanna will even make shoes to your own design.

The owner, Signor Panzarotto, has been active in the business for 45 years, and continues to maintain the same standard of workmanship he demanded many years ago. Today his daughter assists him in carrying on the tradition.

The clientele are mostly habitués, some of whom have been coming for as long as 40 years. They include several of Rome's top social leaders. A number of clients from Australia, the United States, and Scandinavia are accustomed to ordering their shoes through the mail.

The prices of course are considerably higher than they once were. Ready-made shoes for women are $23 to $105; ready-made shoes for men are $30 to $49; made-to-measure shoes sell for $30 and up. Shoes for men and women may be purchased in either ready-to-wear or made-to-measure. Custom-made shoes take one to two weeks to make ready.

Handbags also are available ready-made or made-to-order at prices ranging from $26 on up.

Sanna looks like a simple cozy shoe shop. But the clientele who come here are confident that what they buy will be equal to or better than that of the most elegant-looking salons. The Romans, in their choice of possessions, have always valued quality above all else. The success of Sanna proves it.

SHOES FOR MEN AND WOMEN—ROME

Fragiacomo

Via Condotti 35
Rome
Telephone: 688–780

Open daily except Sunday
7½% discount
Medium high

This newcomer to the fashionable Via Condotti is already well-known in the North of Italy. Fragiacomo has been selling shoes to well-shod Milanese and Turinese for more than 20 years now, and the brand also is sold at select shops in the United States.

Fragiacomo is not only the name of a shoe salon—it is also a brand name of a line of shoes. But Fragiacomo stores carry only their own designs.

The men's shoes are well-made, designed with up-to-date (but not extreme) styling. The large selection of women's shoes ranges from sporty sandals to elegant dress boots. We thought that this store's most outstanding merchandise was its line of appliquéed evening boots for women (about $50). These white kid boots are knee-high, and decorated with beaded flowers and exotic designs. The manager, Signor Andrea, tells us the boots are a specialty of the shop.

Prices are on the medium side for Rome. Men's shoes run from $23 to $34, women's shoes from $20 to $30. Alligator naturally runs higher, about $50 for women. Boots sell for between $40 and $50.

One word of caution: Italian shoes are made on different lasts than American styles. No one seems to know just what sort of feet they fit best, but there are many American feet they simply do not fit well. So before you buy a pair of shoes, be sure to walk around and try them out.

Signor Andrea, the manager, is himself on hand to see that the clientele is well served. The shop is unusually busy and bustling, but the attention is personal.

PALAZZI

Via Borgognona 7C
Rome
Telephone: 689–143

Open daily except Sunday
10% discount
Medium high

Rome has a reputation for excellent men's tailoring, and Palazzi contributes to that reputation.

The firm is a relative newcomer to the city's clothiers, for it has only been in business since 1964. But among well-clad Romans, it's known as a place to buy men's-wear that's fashionably styled yet refined *(raffinate* they call it). It has up-to-date taste that's tempered with moderation.

That's to say that Palazzi swings—but just a little—enough so that a businessman wearing one of their suits will look respectable enough for his job at the bank or corporation, yet distinctive enough to continue on to one of Rome's fashionable supper spots that evening.

They're the kind of clothes that selective American men like, too. In fact, Palazzi's styles have been so enthusiastically received by American buyers that the firm plans to open its own shop in New York City during the coming year.

The Rome boutique is large and inviting. It's filled with ready-to-wear of all sorts—shirts, coats, suits, ties, sweaters, and shoes. In addition, there's a large selection of materials that will be custom-made into suits. The men's fabrics, whether in bolts or ready-made apparel, were, we thought, unusually handsome.

Prices are reasonable for merchandise of such fine quality.

Ready-to-wear suits are about $125; overcoats run between $110 and $260; made-to-measure suits cost between $170 and $200, shirts between $14 and $36, and shoes between $30 and $36.

If you've always had a desire to try Italian tailoring, but have been fearful of the extremes to which the tailoring can go, Palazzi's ready-to-wear might suit you best. Distinctive, yes. Extreme, no.

MEN'S-WEAR—ROME

peluso

Via del Corso 10
Rome
Telephone: 673-686

Open daily except Sunday
10% discount
Medium

When you check into your hotel room and discover that you forgot your ties in Paris...When the laundry mangles the only shirt that matches your pin-stripe suit...When the weather turns chilly and you don't have a sweater...head for Peluso.

Peluso is a fine place to stock up on whatever you've forgotten. For this men's-wear shop offers a good selection at moderate prices. The styling is up-to-date, but not extreme.

Peluso has been serving Romans at this same location for 35 years now, with the business remaining in the same family.

The specialties here are ready-made shirts and ties. Shirts with long sleeves sell from $11 to $16. Summer shirts are priced from $7.50 on up. Ties cost between $4 and $8. There are sweaters from $11 to $19, and summer slacks for about $11. You'll also see raincoats priced about $55, coats from $55 to $120, and suits from $72 to $112.

Much of the merchandise that Peluso sells are items with internationally known brand names. Well-made and not high-style, they have a distinct appeal to Roman professional men, and are sound values. For everyday furnishings and accessories of fine quality, Peluso wins high marks.

MEN'S CUSTOM TAILORING—ROME

Marcello Prageldi

Via Milano 51
Rome
Telephone: 481-538

Open daily except Sunday
15% discount
Medium

Marcello Prageldi is a Roman tailor. He's a fine Roman tailor, and although he's only 35 years old, he has already built up a following that includes government officials, lawyers, and journalists. He also makes uniforms of impeccable fit for Italian military officers.

Signor Prageldi has been working with needle and thread ever since the age of 12 when he began as an apprentice tailor. Something of a prodigy in his field, he opened his own business at the age of 21. But instead of working out of a regular shop, he has outfitted a third-floor apartment in the center of Rome as his fitting rooms.

Since there's no shop as such, it's difficult to learn about Prageldi. Yet the list of customers keeps growing, because the Signor is noted for quality work at reasonable prices. Satisfied customers tell friends and the friends become customers.

If you've ever considered having a suit custom-made, you might want to try Prageldi. Suits can be made for you on order within 5 days, and cost between $105 and $125 depending on the fabric.

There's a large selection of English and Italian materials to choose from, and shirts, too, are made-to-measure for about $15 each.

In addition to the custom-made merchandise, you'll find a fine selection of ready-to-wear shirts, ties, and cashmere sweaters.

One word of caution: some Italian styles are avant-garde by American standards, so select carefully. Signor Prageldi, even though he speaks no English, is a master of sign language, and can help you choose wisely.

CHILDREN'S CLOTHING—ROME

la cicogna

Via Frattina 138
Rome
Telephone: 671–912

Open daily except Sunday
10% discount
Medium to medium high

Need a bib, a layette, a blanket? How about embroidered leggings for a tomboy? Want an elegant suède fur-trimmed coat for that young lady of 9? How about some funny pajama bags to bring to the youngsters back home? Or are you in urgent need of diaper service?

Whatever you're looking for in children's wear and furnishings, from infants to age 10, La Cicogna is sure to have it. There appears to be no end to the variety of merchandise tucked away in this two-story shop. On one typical day, we found 40 differently styled and priced coats for a child age 6. And if that's not enough, the shop also offers a baby-sitting service, American-type diaper service—and even maternity clothes.

The Via Frattina shop actually is one of a corporate-owned chain of 50 children's shops throughout Italy. Signor John Puccio, who began the operation in 1953, is responsible for this organization's phenomenal growth. Signor Puccio understands his customers and sets high standards for the products he sells. Although there are many shops, each one has the characteristics of an exclusive establishment.

Italian families, no matter what their income level, spend considerably more on children's clothes than do their American counterparts, and they demand quality. Roman children always seem to be beautifully dressed. It is not at all unusual to see a Roman matron, who spends $40 on a dress for herself, spend the same amount on a dress for her 3-year-old daughter.

For this reason, the prices at La Cicogna may vary widely, but the merchandise all has in common its excellent quality and styling. We could find no slipshod workmanship or shoddy materials anywhere. Whether you spend $2 or $200, the shop claims to stand behind its merchandise.

The clientele is about 70 percent Italian and 30 percent foreign. There are 8 such shops in Rome proper. Since the one on Via Frattina is most centrally located and several of the staff speak English, we would recommend you shop here.

In Florence, La Cicogna is located on Via della Vigna Nuova 76R.

And in case you haven't guessed by now, *La Cicogna* means "The Stork."

LEATHER BAGS—FLORENCE

Dupre

Piazza Signoria 5
Florence
Telephone: 262-790

Open daily except Sunday
10% discount

Dupre truly is a find.

And like many finds, you have to be told about it, for it is tucked away on the second floor (three flights up) of a totally inconspicuous building where you would never chance upon it.

Dupre is a handbag factory. But it is a very special one, for it turns out bags of only top-quality leather and workmanship. If you love fine leather, you will fully appreciate Dupre's fine selection.

Because it's a factory, the establishment naturally has no color or charm, but it does offer an excellent opportunity to save money on handbags that usually appear for sale only in the finer shops of Europe and America.

The merchandise is on display in a small front office. When we were there, only the more classic styles were on view. The newest line, which is more high fashion, was stored on shelves. So if you don't see what you want immediately, be sure to ask.

Signora Carla, the co-owner of the shop, is a charming Swiss who speaks perfect English. She is proud of her products and will be delighted to discuss them with you. If you can't communicate in Italian, it's best to phone before coming up to make sure the Signora is there. Her partner and the rest of the help speak no English.

The leathers, as Signora Carla will explain to you, are mostly imports; the best leathers from Germany and France go into the making of these bags. The imported ostrich is beautiful.

Open a patent leather bag, for example, and you're likely to find it lined inside with a suède that's of as fine a quality as the outside of the bag. And it all smells deliciously leathery. The clasps and attachments are interestingly detailed.

Dupre develops and shows a new collection twice a year. While the styling stays fashionably up-to-date, it's not the sort of design that will look outdated after one season. A Dupre bag, we find, looks as good the third year you own it as it does the first.

C. Spulcioni

Via Calimala 10R
Florence
Telephone: 21-526

Open daily except Sunday
12% discount
Medium to medium high

There are lots of fine leather shops in Florence, but Spulcioni is one of the favorites of Florentine women. That's because the quality, the styling, the large selection, and the prices all add up to a pleasing buy.

This small, jam-packed shop carries a large selection of medium-priced bags in all shapes, sizes, and colors. The styling, up-to-date without being extreme, is designed to fit women of varying sizes and ages. There are tiny bags for small girls, swinging shoulder-strap bags for young sophisticates, and elegant suède and alligator for well-to-do Florentine matrons. The prices vary accordingly. Handbags sell for anywhere from $24 to $300. However, you'll find a very large selection in the $25-$40 range. Wallets sell for between $2 and $24, and they make excellent gifts to take to friends.

Signor Spulcioni knows how to select quality leather. He's been working with leather for 45 years now, and like many a local boy, he learned about quality and workmanship by apprenticing as a youngster to one of the city's numerous leather workrooms. About 25 years ago, he decided to strike out on his own, and opened the business which, over the years, has built up a substantial following. The little shop is located in a busy section of town, just opposite the straw market.

One of the shop's specialties, more popular among tourists (Italian visitors and foreigners alike) than among Florentines, is "Florentine leather goods"—those handbags and wallets that you find imprinted with the gold fleur-de-lis, the symbol of Florence. You'll find similar-looking merchandise around the town, but at Spulcioni's we thought the quality was generally superior.

CLEMENTE

Via Calzaivoli 10
Florence
Telephone: 298-749 or 276-195

Open daily except Sunday
15% discount
Medium high to high

When sunny Italy becomes damp and drizzly, that's the time to head for Clemente.

This long-time umbrella manufacturer has been keeping Florentines dry ever since 1870. Indeed, in 1906, Clemente umbrellas won a gold medal for design in London—and that's saying a lot since umbrella designs haven't been much improved on in the past 100 years.

The umbrellas, for both men and women, come in traditional designs and are extremely well-made. There are long elegant types, short portable ones that fit into a suitcase, and collapsible umbrellas with leather cases. The prices run between $6.50 and $65, and those in the higher range are the kind that last a lifetime.

Now that you're dry, take a look at Clemente's leather goods, as well. The leather merchandise displays the same fine workmanship and quality of materials and classic design as do the umbrellas. Some of the handbags Clemente manufactures itself; others are purchased from workrooms whose standards are in keeping with those of the shop.

There are briefcases for men at $26 to $100, as well as a large selection of luggage, belts, and wallets. The handbags for women, of elegant traditional styling, sell for $30 and up. You'll find beautiful alligator bags here, too.

The décor of the shop tells you a great deal about the principles on which the business is operated and the kind of merchandise you can expect. The old-fashioned showcases of dark wood and the lighting fixtures that date back to an earlier time combine to create an aura of elegance, distinction, and assured quality. And that's what the merchandise is like.

Madova GLOVES

Via Guicciardini 1R, also 31R
Florence
Telephone: 298-655

Open daily except Sunday, regular winter hours,
summer 9:00 A.M.–8:00 P.M.

10% discount
Medium

In Florence, successful commerce and skilled craftsmanship frequently go hand-in-hand, and the customer benefits. Madova Gloves is a perfect example. Its two small shops, located almost next door to each other, have a constant stream of customers, Italians during the winter and foreign visitors in summer.

Madova's success is due to its fine designs, quality workmanship, and favorable prices. By American standards, the prices are incredibly low. And small wonder, for Madova is the only glove shop-factory in Florence that both makes and sells its own gloves at the source.

The kidskin gloves come in all lengths and colors, lined and unlined, embroidered and plain. Prices run between $2.25 and $10.00, with most of the merchandise in the $4 to $6 range. The highest price is for above-the-elbow white wedding gloves.

Men's gloves are sold here, too. They come in leather with fur lining, as well as in dressy suède—all selling for between $4 and $6.

Signor Donnini, the proprietor, is proud of his products. He often takes time out from his work to show a visitor exactly how a pair of gloves is prepared and sewn together. A good glove, explains the Signor, stretches horizontally across the hand, never vertically, and he then demonstrates that his gloves do just that.

He should know. Signor Donnini's grandfather worked for a glove factory. His father started the Madova factory, which lasted until 1929 (when the U.S. depression ended the export business on which it thrived). Two sons reopened the factory in 1946, and in 1948 the first of the two shops opened.

Today, the Signor points with pride to a leather montage hanging on the wall made up of labels from dozens of the larger and better shops in the United States to which Madova sells in quantity.

SUMMER AND CRUISE WEAR—FLORENCE

Paola Davitti

Via Maggio 13
Florence
Telephone: 261–341

Open daily except Sunday
10% discount

Paola Davitti is a splendid success story. Only 8 short years ago, she was working as a secretary. Then one day she decided that her real talent lay in designing clothes. So she opened a small, one-room, rooftop boutique that consisted of a sewing machine, a tiny office, and two employees. Today, she owns one of the best and most unusual high-fashion establishments in Florence, employs more than 400 persons, and sells her line of ready-to-wear to better shops around the world.

Signora Davitti's designs are young. They're gay. They're colorful. They're for summer and cruise wear. The outfits, the pants suits, blouses, dresses, and evening wear, are all made from silk scarves—but these are special scarves, original prints that the Signora designs herself. They are stylized prints, mostly floral, occasionally geometric. Fourteen different prints in 14 different color combinations go into a season's wardrobe.

Now the Signora is making bathing suits and tops—and with such success that there are sure to be more of them in the future.

Davitti has no winter line. "I have no feeling for winter," says the Signora. "Summer is the season I love."

The business operation is housed on the first floor (one flight up) of a fifteenth-cenutry building on a street that runs parallel to Via Guicciardini. The Davitti boutique also is housed here, so when you enter, be sure to ask for the boutique. Several of the personnel speak English.

The range of prices is wide and surprisingly reasonable for the quality of the merchandise. Sizes run from 8 to 16. As you may have guessed by the designs, these outfits look best on the smaller woman.

THE CORNER SHOP
Borgo San Jacopo 29 R/B
Florence
Telephone: 260-803

Open daily except Sunday
10% discount
Medium

The Corner Shop is the type of boutique so popular on New York's swinging East Side and in London's Chelsea district. It's hip. It's chic. And though it's something new for Florence, stylish younger Florentines are already turning it into a favorite local institution.

The Corner Shop is for the young—not necessarily for the young in age, but for the youthful in looks. It features fashionable ready-to-wear at moderate prices. Some of the clothes can be quite elegant. Others are for fun. All are well-made.

A specialty of the shop is knitwear, and knit dresses sell for about $25. Other dresses are between $15 and $50. Suits and coats are priced between $65 and $115, and silk blouses, shirts, and slacks cost between $8 and $25.

You'll also find fun furs (in winter), lounging pajamas, pants outfits, and accessories. The colors and prints of the fabrics are interesting, and in tune with the styling.

The décor of The Corner Shop is simple, which is just as well, because the place is smallish like the other shops alongside it on the narrow Via San Jacopo. The merchandise, however, is well displayed for easy viewing.

The shop opened its doors in 1966, recent for Florence, a city in which many merchants can count back through several generations. But the owner of the boutique, Piero Canovai, and his family have long been in the business of producing women's apparel. Many of the items in the shop are designed and manufactured by the family factory and are sold under the brand names of Caroline, Tricot, and Jasmine. So this is not a new venture—just a new look. The Corner Shop can outfit you with a new look, too—a look that's smart and contemporary.

Ricami di Firenze

Via Tornabuoni 18R
Florence
Telephone: 284-836

Open daily except Sunday
10% discount
Medium high

Ever longed to luxuriate in flowing, silken-soft lingerie? Ricami can easily satisfy that longing for you. Smart Florentine women have been buying here for years. They know that, though the prices may be a bit on the high side, the quality of the merchandise is impeccable.

The design, the delicate embroidery, the fanciful detailing, all contrive to make the wearer feel deliciously feminine.

The décor contributes to that mood, as well. It is a very feminine-looking boutique even from the outside. The large windows are decorated with fresh flower arrangements and samples of the merchandise. Inside, the shop is bright, airy, elegant, and very female. A man might find this atmosphere a bit overpowering, but women adore it.

There are frivolous nighties, flowing peignoirs, lacy slips, delicate hankies, and luxurious robes. There are lots of silk, fine cotton, high-quality synthetics, and softest wool. Almost everything is handmade and treated with the same high craftsmanship that has always characterized Florentine lingerie and linens.

Ricami also makes beautiful hand-embroidered sheets and pillowcases, some with decorations, some with monograms. Florentine ladies have been filling their hope chests with these for years. But we don't know whether we'd recommend them for American washing machines—the materials are so good, they'd probably survive nicely, but somehow the thought of that intricate embroidery on a spin-cycle is incongruous.

All lingerie is specially designed for the shop. There is also a good selection of ready-to-wear, take-with-you merchandise available. And Ricami specializes in made-to-order, too.

The clientele includes many foreign visitors as well as Florentines. A good number of travelers continue to order regularly from Ricami, even after having returned home.

FASHION IN LEATHER—FLORENCE

Luisa Fuiano Boccuzzi

Piazza della Signoria 3 (one flight up)
Florence
Telephone: 294-496

Open daily except Sunday
12% discount
Expensive

Boccuzzi is not for the fainthearted.

The prices can be substantial, the atmosphere is that of a rather elegant and formal salon, and the service is highly personalized. The clientele are almost entirely well-to-do Italians who like this aura.

However, if you appreciate beautifully styled and tailored leather outfits for both men and women, you, too, should visit this salon.

The Boccuzzi designs are high-styled, distinctive, and elegant. In 1967, the designer line was awarded the "Oscar" for *Alta Moda in Pèlle*—high fashion in leather.

On our visit, we especially liked a woman's brown leather coat lined with white Mongolian lamb for contrast—the price: $260. We also were impressed by a beautiful embroidered suède pants outfit that sold for $240. For men, we especially fancied a leather safari suit that cost $153.

Of course, many items sell for less and some sell for more. Dresses start at about $75, women's coats at $137. Men's leather jackets sell for $75. Men's coats vary in price depending on the styling and leather—a reversible lined leather coat is $300. Your *Discovery* Card can provide a substantial saving here, even though the original prices are themselves considerably lower than the cost of comparable merchandise back home.

If you see something you like, and it fits, you can take it with you. The variety on display is substantial. If what you want is not available in your size, it can usually be made within a week.

English is not spoken here, but you'll find the personnel most attentive. Either Signora Boccuzzi or her head designer is usually at the salon to serve you.

UMBERTO ZANOBETTI

Via Calimala 18–22R
Florence
Telephone: 270-646

Open daily except Sunday
10% discount
Medium high

In a twelfth-century building, complete with frescoes on the walls, the Zanobetti brothers run one of the most successful men's and women's boutiques in Florence.

Although the building is old, the shop's outlook is new. For Zanobetti capitalizes on the growing trend toward ready-to-wear, an old habit for Americans but a new one for Italians.

The three floors of this large shop are filled with ready-made clothing and smartly dressed young Italians, who more and more are drawn to this type of dress. If you enter the establishment early in the morning, the atmosphere is that of a sedate, long-established clothier. But if you return at 6:00 on a Saturday evening, especially in winter, you might think a bargain sale was in progress—there are that many customers milling about, and clothes are being tried on in profusion.

Another reason for the large number of customers is that Italians are as individualistic as other people. Though Florentine fashions are considered chic abroad, the fashionable Florentine likes to have something different, too. In this case that something is a French import. Zanobetti carries such French names as Dior and Cardin, all in ready-to-wear. And the prices, we're told, are slightly lower than in Paris because they don't include the heavy French taxes.

Of course, there's also plenty of local merchandise. The store carries its own exclusive designs as well as those of other designers. Lest you think that Zanobetti is a new business, we should tell you that they have been tailoring and selling clothes to Florentines for three generations, ever since 1902.

The clothes carry a fairly wide range of prices. Men's suits sell for $75 to $200, men's overcoats from $90 to $300, men's shirts from $12 to $40, and ties from $4 to $11.50. Women's dresses are priced at $30 to $75, women's sweaters—including cashmere—from $15 to $40, and suits from $57 to $112.

Overall the merchandise consists of wearable, up-to-date fashion with an international flair.

SHOES FOR MEN AND WOMEN—FLORENCE

Raspini

Via Martelli 5/7R (also at Via Porta Santa Maria 72R)
Florence
Telephone: 298–336

Open daily except Sunday
10% discount
Medium

La Scarpa Che Fa Epoca—Shoes That Make History.

That's Raspini's motto. Too grandiose a claim? Florentines don't think so.

Is this not the shop that recently won the coveted "Oscar d'Oro" award for the best style and quality shoes in all Italy?

Is it not the shop which for half a century has been selling height-of-fashion shoes to sophisticated and well-to-do Italians?

Is it not a shop much in vogue with pace-setting 18-to-35-year-old Florentines?

Is it not a shop so confident of its taste that it sells only its own designs and no one else's?

It is all of these things. And as a result, this small but busy boutique is noted all over Italy.

Shoe boxes are crammed into every available space, and manager Franco Ferrini and his eight salesmen are almost always busy waiting on customers.

It's quality you come here for, and you'll find it in abundance, Both inside the shoes and out, the leather is soft and pliable, and the trims are handsomely fashioned. Considering the style and workmanship, prices are reasonable, too. Shoes for women cost between $12 and $22, for men between $17 and $27.

Raspini is divided into two sections, with the main salesroom devoted to women's shoes and a side alcove reserved for gentlemen's shoes—a good way for each of you to make your own decisions, without back-seat driving from the other. Whichever style you buy, you're practically assured of being a pace-setter back home for several months to come.

Thanks to *La Scarpa Che Fa Epoca*.

SHOES FOR MEN AND WOMEN—FLORENCE

Via Degli Spezial 10R and Via Porta Rossa 14R
Florence
Telephone: 276-535

Open daily except Sunday
10% discount
Medium

In a nation where shoes are noted for their high-fashion styling, Romano takes the more classic approach. In a city where elegance is the keynote, Romano adds a relaxing touch. It's an approach that has paid off.

Romano's shoes are casual and comfortable, just like the shop itself. You'll feel at home here, in an easygoing atmosphere and a somewhat rustic décor. And you might well find shoes to feel at home with, as well.

Now don't get the idea that these are what the English used to call sturdy walking shoes. They're not. They're very much in the contemporary *mòda*. But at the same time, they're comfortable enough to provide a welcome change if you've been out sightseeing for days and your feet have had about all they can stand.

Prices? As at so many other shoe boutiques in Florence, they're altogether reasonable—about $16 to $25 for women's shoes, $21 to $30 for men's shoes. One reason for these modest prices, we discovered, is that Romano not only does its own styling but makes all its own products, so pays no outside designer or middleman.

We noticed a fine selection of matching handbags as well, also made by Romano's own craftsmen.

It's important that you understand that Romano's are not "sporty" shoes. Casual in Florence doesn't mean quite the same thing as it does at home. So let's say that, not being sporty and not being high fashion, the styles at Romano are somewhere in between: comfortable enough to do the Boboli Gardens and walk the museums in, elegant enough to wear to dinner at a fine restaurant. A good compromise, and one of the factors that makes Romano's a popular place with visitors as well as Florentines.

MEN'S-WEAR—FLORENCE

H. Neuber

Via Strozzi 32R
Florence
Telephone: 282-329

Open daily except Sunday
10% discount
Medium to high

Florentines point with pride to H. Neuber.

This is the firm that during the late nineteenth and early twentieth century was an official supplier to the Italian Royal Court—the House of Savoy.

What does it take to become the appointed supplier to royalty? It takes an unsullied reputation for excellence—for quality, reliability, and taste. That same reputation continues to gain the firm the best of clientele today.

Today, the royal court is no more, but the firm continues to attract modern royalty to Florence. Politicians, businessmen, and theater people from other cities stop regularly to be outfitted here.

The merchandise might well be described as elegantly conservative. It's the sort of tailoring, a Florentine friend told us, in which a Fiat corporate officer or a General Motors executive would feel comfortable.

That's not to imply that Neuber is old-fashioned. Quite the contrary. The merchandise stays up-to-date, and the selection contains the best of Italian tailoring, as well as certain exclusive imports from England and France.

The selection is large. The main floor displays shirts, ties, silk robes, underwear, slacks, raincoats, sweaters, in short everything to outfit a gentleman from tip to toe. The suits are mostly of Italian make, the raincoats are English imports, and many of the ties come from France (Yves St. Laurent ties are an exclusive for the firm in Florence). The prices also have a large range from medium to high with lots in both categories.

On the shop's lower floor are clothes for women—mostly sports clothes of classic design and excellent quality. There are rain and sports coats, sweaters, skirts, and scarves among the selection—both Italian and imports.

As you might suspect, the décor of the shop is traditional—high-ceilinged and beautifully maintained, with gold-trimmed wooden display cases. Here is a shop in which you can buy with confidence.

What to Bring Home: More Shopping Discoveries

What to Bring Home: More Shopping Discoveries

The "Made in Italy" label on a product, today, implies a certain kind of quality—fine handiwork, excellent materials, the craftsmanship of skilled artisans, and inventive creative design.

For you, the traveler, it means good buys in furniture, linens, silver, ceramics, jewelry, fabrics, and native handicrafts of all types.

All these products can be found in Rome. The nation's capital presents a vast assortment of specialties from every region of Italy. The prices may be slightly higher than what you would pay in the local region, but it's all together here, beautifully displayed, and—if your wallet or purse can afford it—easy to purchase.

There is modern furniture that comes from Milan and the North. The woods and fabrics are exquisite, the lines are stark and simple, and the workmanship is first-rate. Since the early 1960's, the home furnishings industry in northern Italy has mushroomed to a point where Italian furniture is now among the most sought after in the world. It's expensive, too.

There are crafts that come from the South of Italy and Sardinia. You'll find colorful pottery made in traditional patterns which have been passed on from generation to generation. You'll find intricately woven rugs and blankets that represent weeks of labor.

There are hand-embroidered linens that come from Tuscany. They're made in convents, on farms, and in workshops scattered all over the region.

There are soft silks and stiff brocades, fabrics made in the North, which still bear the patterns of the Renaissance and the Baroque.

There is hand-wrought silverware designed for the home. Italy boasts of a long tradition of silversmiths, which began with the fifteenth century and continues to this very day.

There is marble which comes from the works around Carrara and the quarries in the Aquan Alps. You'll find the stone made into chess sets, vases, bowls, and all kinds of furniture.

There is fine jewelry, some of it antique, much of it original, and all of it hand-wrought. Many of the pieces are inspired by the historical periods of Italy's past—the Etruscan, the Roman, the medieval. And there are modern designs that possess a futuristic look.

If you want a good sampling of what's available, a walk through several of Rome's main shopping streets—Via Condotti, Via Borgognona, Via Frattina, Via della Vite, Via Sistina, and Via del Babuino—should quickly provide it.

You can also see a permanent exhibition of artisan work from all over Italy set up at Via Lincoln 1 EUR. The nation's crafts are on display here.

If you're traveling to Florence, by all means have a look at the local specialties. These include products of linen, leather, straw, paper, gold, and silver.

Leather, which is made up in large quantity for fashion items, also appears in the form of boxes, baskets, furniture decoration, and luggage.

Hand-embroidered linens come in a wide variety of colors, patterns, and prices. Look for tablecloths, embroidered table mats, bed linens, towels, and lingerie.

Linen and leather goods can be found along and near such shopping streets as Via Tornabuoni, Via Calzaiuoli, Via Roma, Via Calimala, and Por. S. Maria.

Goldsmiths, silversmiths, and jewelers are still found on the Ponte Vecchio bridge, where they have been plying their trades for hundreds of years. The variety of merchandise displayed on this small bridge is dazzling. Florentine gold jewelry frequently comes in a satin finish called *satinato*, which gives a brushed look. Filigree work is another specialty.

(Several of the shops at which Florentines make their own purchases are described on the following pages.)

Straw and raffia can be found at the outdoor straw market near the Ponte Vecchio. (This is one place where you are expected to bargain.) A good shop for straw products is Emilio Paoli, Via della Vigna Nuova 24–28, which carries all kinds of objects in straw, such as place mats, flowers, handbags, and even dresses.

For antique-style Italian paper, be sure to visit the shop of Giulio Giannini and Figlio at Piazza Pitti 37R. You'll find notebooks, and boxes in varying shapes, all covered with the decorative delicately patterned paper. The Florentine paper also is sold in individual sheets, which make unusual gift wraps.

Merchants in Rome and particularly in Florence are quite accustomed to dealing with travelers, and will gladly ship your purchases, no matter how large or small. In Florence, several shops offer to take orders during the summertime for delivery as gifts at Christmas.

One word of caution: Italians themselves are extremely quality-conscious and are willing to pay for the best. In fact, the only drawback to some Italian home furnishings is that they often appear to last forever! Many Italian merchants are convinced, however, that Americans would rather pay a little less and not receive quite as much quality. Consequently, you may find, during the summer travel season, that shops emphasize their less expensive items. If you like what you see, that's fine. But if you're looking for something better, and you don't see what you want, be sure to ask for it. The finer shops always do have their more expensive merchandise around, even though it may not be on view.

FINE JEWELRY—ANTIQUE AND ORIGINAL—ROME

Roberto Cecconi

Via del Pellegrino 95
Rome
Telephone: 650–577

Open daily except Sunday
20% discount on jewelry
Medium to medium high

Cecconi looks like an ordinary jewelry shop on the outside. But looks are deceiving.

For Signor Cecconi, who once was a sculptor, now sculpts in gold, and the works that result are some of the most attractive and unusual pieces of jewelry to be found in Rome.

Cecconi's customers are primarily well-to-do Romans who are attracted by the original designs and beautiful quality of his jewelry. Many are loyal devotees who return each year to add a new piece to their personal collections.

As his medium, the Signor uses pure gold, alone or set with precious rubies, emeralds, or pearls. He has developed a special technique for working the gold to create scultpured bas-reliefs— the design is hammered out from the underside of the gold panel. The raised figures that appear are often inspired by ancient Etruscan art. When these gold decorative panels are combined with pearls, the results are striking.

Not a day passes that the Signor isn't thinking about some new design. His jewelry may have an abstract modernistic look at one time. At another time, it may involve such objects as graceful deer, horses, and birds, appearing much as they did in an original seventh-century B.C. work. No two pieces are identical.

Some representative prices: When we were there, a pair of long, hand-carved gold earrings, in Etruscan design, was selling for $209. A pearl and gold pair in modern design was $80. A wide bracelet of gold lacework, inlaid with tiny emeralds and rubies, cost $270. A thinner gold bracelet with a delicate working was $177.

In necklaces, a simple handmade gold chain sells for between $56 and $113. A large rope necklace of gold and pearls is $290. Rings are between $40 and $75, and men's cuff links cost between $35 and $45. Signor Cecconi also collects and sells antique jewelry, as well as some silver (the *Discovery* discount on silver is 10%).

The shop is located 1600 feet from the Piazza Navonne, and within walking distance of St. Peter's. It's a bit away from the usual shopping areas. But one of Rome's master goldsmiths is worth going out of your way to see.

ANGELETTI

Via Condotti 11A
Rome
Telephone: 673–700

Open daily except Sunday
10% discount
Medium to medium high

For over 30 years now, Signor Angeletti and son have been selling fine jewelry, silver, glass ware, and china in this shop on the Via Condotti. During that time, they have not only built up a reputation for quality and reliability, but have developed a very devoted clientele among knowledgeable Romans.

If you like the traditional look in jewelry and silver, you'll find Angeletti's a particularly good place to buy gifts. The items carried here are of a considerable variety and price range. In the area of jewelry, for instance, you'll find watches, charms, enamel bracelets, rings, as well as earrings, necklaces, and bracelets of gold and precious stones. The watches range in price from $12 to $325. Rings sell for the same prices—from $12 to $325.

For the home, there is silverware, silverplate, fine china and glassware, malachite and lapis lazuli ware, Chinese jade and sculpture, silver picture frames, clocks and desk barometers. The clocks, by the way, range from $25 to $325 and make superb wedding gifts.

The décor of the shop is conservative yet attractive. Its showcases and shelves of gleaming glass, framed in highly shellacked wood, combine to give it an aura of stability and confidence. The location of the shop on the Via Condotti contributes further to this aura. The service is excellent and English is spoken by some of the staff.

No wonder that so many Romans say that Angeletti is the traditional jeweler-gift shop at its best.

FINE JEWELRY AND MARBLE WORK—ROME

FONTINALIA

Via Vittoria 12
Rome
Telephone: 688-255

Open daily except Sunday
15% discount
Medium to medium high

It sometimes seems that every time the Romans build an underground garage, dig a building foundation, or put in a new road, they come upon Etruscan remains. Immediately all work is halted, the archeologists move in and excavate, and a new museum room must be added to house the findings. For the Etruscans, those mysterious precursors of the Romans about whom so little is known, left behind some of the most beautiful art objects of the ancient world.

These same objects are being recreated today at Fontinalia, along with outstanding Egyptian and Greco-Roman designs. Gold and marble—both precious materials for the ancients—are found side-by-side in this unusual shop.

Here you will see Etruscan jewelery, exactly copied and reproduced in precious gold and jewels. There are bracelets, rings, and pins, in designs so ancient that they look surprisingly contemporary. The gold is intricately worked and detailed, yet the Etruscan patterns are abstract. (Prices: about $60 for a ring; $100 for a pin.)

Here, too, you will find reproductions of antique statues, gargoyles, fountains, and outdoor scultpure, all done in Carrara marble. The works are perfect for outdoor gardens, especially of the formal type.

Fontinalia owns its own quarry, so the prices of marble works are extremely favorable. In addition to the outdoor pieces, occasional contemporary pieces are made for sale (such as a marble chess set and chessboard priced at $70).

The name of the shop comes from *Fontinalia*—a festival that was celebrated in ancient Rome in honor of Fonto, the patron god of wells and fountains.

WMf *atelier*

Piazzo Di Spagna 82–83
Rome
Telephone: 672–294

Open daily except Sunday and Monday morning
10% discount
Medium to medium high

What's a German shop that specializes in contemporary tablewares doing near Rome's Spanish Steps?

Well—several things.

First of all, it's partially the result of Italy and Germany both belonging to the Common Market, which means that the imported merchandise sells at favorable prices in Rome.

Second, it's an indicator of the changing tastes of well-to-do Romans. When WMF first opened its doors in 1966, the big question was whether the tradition-minded, antique-oriented Romans would accept what is among the most modern flatware and glassware in Western Europe.

The answer came almost immediately—a resounding yes! We were led to this shop by several young Romans who do much of their shopping here and point to their acquisitions with pride.

WMF in Rome is the retail outlet for the German factory which began operation in 1856. At the end of World War II, it was the first European factory to develop a contemporary line of flatware.

The flatware is available in stainless steel, silver plate, and sterling. There also are stainless steel serving plates which make excellent gifts. If you're interested in a substantial purchase, you'll find a 75-piece service for 12 will cost between $100 and $140 in stainless steel.

The WMF fine crystal glassware costs between $2.50 and $3.50 per glass, and the lines are elegant and simple. A distinctive crystal vase can be purchased for about $25.

In addition to their own brand, the shop also carries Italian china and other gift items satisfying the firm's high design standards. For example, while we were there, we saw a beautfiul hand-crafted jewelry box. The price range and selection at the shop are so wide that you can find a gift item for $4 or $300.

You won't have any difficulty locating WMF either. Its expansive glass front sets off the display inside. Peep through the windows first, and if you like good contemporary lines, you'll be drawn inside to look some more.

The personnel here speak very little English, since most of the clientele are Italian. But the merchandise speaks for itself.

Myricae

Via Frattina 36–34
Rome
Telephone: 675-335

Open daily except Sunday
10% discount
Medium

Signora Massetti, the owner of Myricae, used to be a journalist. Then Mussolini came to power, and she was no longer permitted to write. So the Signora, already considered unusual for being a lady journalist, did something even more startling. In 1929 she and her husband opened the first handicrafts boutique in Rome. Their merchandise—original crafts and ceramics made by Italian peasants and artisans.

More than 40 years have passed, but the Signora and her boutique go on. She still makes scouting trips all over the Italian countryside and brings her finds back to Rome.

Admittedly, some things have changed. Peasant crafts, once considered primitive objects, are now considered desirable decorative accessories by city sophisticates and architects in both Europe and abroad. So, in addition to the local market, the Signora now operates a significant export business.

As more and more Italians leave the farms for the cities, original crafts have become increasingly difficult to obtain. Nevertheless, Myricae still manages to maintain a large, wide-ranging selection of excellent quality. Long-time customers tell us that the merchandise is as attractive as ever.

If you're looking for an inexpensive but impressive gift, you can find an earthenware table service with place settings for 6 for as little as $10. Or if you want something smaller to take back home, there's delightful pottery, gaily colored vases and bowls, and amusing ceramic figurines that can be had for anywhere between $3 and $30. A bright-colored bedspread that comes from Abruzzi and sells for $8 is an excellent buy. For more serious collectors of crafts, the shop has some superb Sardinian tapestries, expensively priced at about $130 to $260.

When you visit the shop, be sure to go upstairs. Some of the most interesting objects we found were hidden on the upper level.

Myricae, a Latin word, is the name of a verse from Virgil that describes a bush that grows in the country. It is a commonplace shrub, but is beautiful, simple, and elegantly proportioned. Myricae's crafts are like that, too.

ARTESTILE

Via Frattina 114
Rome
Telephone: 687–663

Open daily except Sunday
10% discount (excluding "sale" merchandise)
Medium to medium high

Artestile sells china that comes from France, Germany, Czechoslovakia, and Italy. And it carries some of the best-known names from these countries—Limoges, Hutschenreuter, Aschenbarch, and, of course, Italy's own Ginori china.

With a selection like that it's no wonder that this small, busy shop appears a bit cluttered. There's a lot inside. But if you're in the market for European china or you're looking for a gift for the home, it's worth going through.

The shop also has a large selection of crystal, mostly in traditional patterns. The crystal is all of Italian make and is available in stemware and individual gift items.

The price range at Artestile is wide. You can find a 41-piece set of Czechoslovakian china for as little as $37. Or you can buy blue-and-gold-banded French Limoges at $608 for a 56-piece set. And there are many other lines priced in between.

If you've never seen Ginori china, you'll find a representative selection of its traditional patterns here. Ginori can range from simple to ornate, from playful to elegant. We liked an attractive 53-piece set for 12, in geometric pattern, that sold for $60.

Limoges cake platters and cutting knives, priced between $20 and $30, and porcelain occasional pieces also make good gifts.

Artestile is accustomed to wrapping its delicate merchandise carefully for shipment. But if you do decide to mail some back, we suggest you play it safe and insure each package against breakage.

CASA DELL'ALLUMINIO

Piazza S. Silvestro 25–26
Rome
Telephone: 681–756

Open daily except Sunday
10% discount
Medium

If you've ever wondered how Italians make those fantastically shaped noodles and spaghetti, here's where to find out. A single trip to Casa Dell' Alluminio and the secrets of Italian *pasta*-making can be yours.

You could be the first on your block to return home with a Roman *pasta* machine, either the deluxe model that makes eight different kinds of noodle shapes or—if you want to be a bit conservative—the three-shape model.

And of course you might like to accompany that with a Roman coffee grinder and your own one-of-a-kind *espresso* set.

Whatever you need (or want), Casa Dell' Alluminio is ready to serve you as it has served Roman housewives for 60 years.

The *pasta*-makers here range from $11 for the three-shape model to $30 for the deluxe model, with several intermediate units. Hand coffee grinders are priced at $6, while the electric types sell for $6 to $33. *Espresso* coffee-makers of steel cost between $3 and $10; Neapolitan units of aluminum can be bought for under a dollar. There's even a large *Capuccino*-maker of the kind that prepares *espresso* and steamed milk, such as you'll find in Roman coffee bars.

There also are pepper grinders, knives, trays, and hand-decorated, one-of-a-kind *espresso* cups that cost from 50¢ up.

If, while you're browsing through, your husband balks at these items of domesticity, never fear. The Casa has something special to please him, too—an exclusive trouser press. This Italian unit contains a special front panel into which the trousers are inserted overnight; they come out in the morning pressed, as fresh as new.

Signor Pasotti, the proprietor, speaks English and will be happy to show you how any of his shop's merchandise works.

There's no doubt—if you're tired of bringing home the usual tourist items, Casa Dell' Alluminio can change all that. Be an original!

Cassina

Via del Babuino 100
Rome
Telephone: 673–330

Open daily except Sunday
10% discount
Expensive

Italian furniture is gaining increasing stature in the international world of home furnishings. Indeed, many architects and decorators believe that the Italians now create the best modern furnishings in the world. Most of the furniture is manufactured in the North of Italy, near Milan. But a few select shops in Rome carry the lines. Cassina is such a shop.

Many of the designs at Cassina were actually created by the famed architect Le Corbusier, many decades ago, but the lines were so extreme for their time that it took several generations before they could be accepted. Even today, they have a supermodern look to Americans.

Cassina includes, in its showroom, couches and armchairs by Scarpa as well as Le Corbusier. The prices are high—which is to be expected since all the materials used in the manufacture are the best. There are leather, rich rosewood, stainless steel, velvet, and tweed—all of outstanding design and workmanship. Nevertheless, we found the prices considerably lower in Rome than for similar pieces abroad.

A stunning Corbusier chaise longue made of steel and ponyskin costs under $350. A Corbusier chair with steel tubing, and covered in leather, costs about $145.

Scarpa's three-seater couch, made of black leather cushions on a rosewood and leather frame, costs $760. The matching easy chair sells for just under $450.

The Cassina shop, although founded in 1927, is done in a completely modern décor to match the furnishings. The two levels of the shop are sparingly filled, so that each piece of furniture displayed can be seen and appreciated from all angles. Moreover, the back of each chair, couch, and cabinet is as completely finished and detailed as the front.

Cassina's clients are mainly architects, both Italian and foreign. But more and more Roman families are beginning to buy here—to complement their antique treasures with modern furnishings.

MODERN FURNITURE—ROME

ecno

Via del Babuino 155A
Rome
Telephone: 687–441 and 687–442

Open daily except Sunday
10% discount
Expensive

Tecno is another shop on the Via del Babuino in which you can see the latest in contemporary Italian furnishings.

Actually, Tecno is the name of a manufacturer of Italian furniture based in the North of Italy. The Tecno line started in 1952 and was among the first to manufacture modern furniture in any significant quantity in Italy. Today, the line is so successful that it is being sold in almost all the major capitals of Europe. The Rome shop is the retail outlet for central and southern Italy.

Tecno's forte is furniture for the office, although there are designs for the home as well. Indeed, the contemporary and clean lines of the designs make the furnishings appropriate to virtually any environment. By office furniture, we include not only desks and chairs—although there's plenty of that—but also bookshelves, easy chairs, couches, and modern light fixtures. It is elegant furniture, beautifully made of the best woods and metals and fabrics.

The woods appear in vivid colorings—reds and blacks and whites—as well as in the natural tones of rosewood and oak. When it comes to fabrics, there's no limit to the choice.

The factory in the North makes all the furniture in such a way that component parts are packed in relatively small boxes, and are simple to ship and export.

Tecno design and high standards of workmanship were among the factors that began to draw the attention of international decorators and architects to Italy. As one architect friend told us: "The prices are high but the quality is unexcelled. The kind of workmanship that Italians are putting into contemporary furniture is difficult to duplicate anywhere else in the world today."

Persepolis

Via del Babuino 31
Rome
Telephone: 686-647

Open daily except Sunday
10% discount
Expensive

If you're a fancier of Persian carpets, Persepolis offers the opportunity to see an unrivaled display. This 6-year-old establishment is the largest dealer in Persian rugs in the entire Mediterranean area.

The merchandise—both antique and modern—comes directly from the home base in Teheran. For Persepolis was established under the direction of the Iranian Persian Tapestry Center, and sells rugs from every region of that country. When the Rome shop opened its doors, Iranian nobility, including the Shah and Empress Farah Dibah, turned out to give their personal stamp of approval.

The selection and quality are excellent and there are many uncommon types and designs. The carpets are superbly exhibited against marble floors and whitewashed walls, complemented by Persian grillwork. The place glows with colors and patterns. Downstairs, the rooms are built in the form of caves, and here there are precious antiques on view. We saw a beautiful Kashan Imperial of the eighteenth century made of silk, as well as a rare Isphahan made by the Master Serafhian.

The modern rugs are made in ancient patterns and are crafted by hand. The prices on these are fixed, according to size and design.

"Persian carpets have become so popular that many imitations are now being made in Europe," Signor Giuian, the director of the shop, explained to us. "To prevent confusion, the Iranian government has instituted a classification system for original Persian carpets—both modern and antique. Our carpets are all under this classification system, so the customer is assured of what he's buying."

In addition to the main showroom on the Via del Babuino, Persepolis also displays at Vialle della Civilta del Lavoro 110-112.

Between the two, you'll see some of the most interesting wall hangings and floor coverings anywhere this side of the Arabian nights.

A. RISALITI

Ponte Vecchio 27–29R
Florence
Telephone: 294-656

Open daily except Sunday
15% discount
Inexpensive to expensive

The exact age of the famed Ponte Vecchio is unknown. But we do know that during the sixteenth century, Cosimo Medici, ruler of the Florentine Republic, as part of a large public works program, ordered away the butcher stalls that had lined the bridge for decades. The stalls were forcibly upgraded, and ever since that time, jewelers, goldsmiths, and silversmiths have occupied the Ponte Vecchio.

One such jeweler is Risaliti, an establishment that for 100 years has been selling Florentines fine works at good values.

What we liked about Risaliti were the designs of the jewelry. Many of the pieces are hand-worked, delicate and tastefully done. The variety is tremendous—for example, there are 700 different sets of cuff links in the shop. There are rings and bracelets, earrings and necklaces galore. They come in solid gold, gold encrusted with precious stones, or gold decorated with semiprecious materials. There are massive pieces and delicate ones, ornately wrought works or simply carved works. In addition to contemporary designs, Risaliti also does reproductions of antique jewelry—always in gold.

The price range is broad in scope. We saw a gold and coral bracelet for a little girl that sold for $5. We also saw an exquisite diamond and sapphire bracelet for a big girl that sold for thousands of dollars.

Whomever you have in mind for a gift of jewelry, you'll undoubtedly find a piece at Risaliti that suits your price range and taste. Cuff links for men are available for $35 and up. There's a good assortment of rings for under $100. Bracelets and pins start at $20.

Signora Albertina Risaliti runs the shop and is there regularly to make sure that the clientele are properly served. Several members of her staff speak English.

All the stones, gold, and workmanship are guaranteed to the customer in writing.

F.lli Piccini

Ponte Vecchio 23R
Florence
Telephone: 294–768

Open daily except Sunday
12% discount
Inexpensive to expensive

Piccini is another of the master jewelers who call the Ponte Vecchio home. The brothers Piccini have occupied their spot since 1936. When the floods hit the bridge in 1966, the old shop was smashed by timbers that ripped through the bridge, and practically washed it away. Today, however, it's business as usual—with one difference: the new store is light and bright, while the original shop had an almost medieval quality to it.

Piccini is located in the middle of the bridge, so when you enter you'll be treated to a beautiful view that overlooks the River Arno. The ground-level showroom is for jewelry, while silver is shown on the upper level.

The Piccini brothers have several specialties—they sell antique silver and original antique jewelry as well as modern works. Almost all the contemporary pieces are designed by Armando Piccini himself, who proudly tells us that, in 1958, his firm won the "Diamonds International Award" in New York—a coveted prize. We wouldn't doubt it, for we found many of the works in the shop practically irresistible.

Like many Italian businesses, this one is family-run. Right now, a grandfather, three sons, and one grandson are all working together. With so many relatives in the business, you can be sure the standards of workmanship and quality are being closely watched.

Taste in jewelry is a very personal thing. But it was our feeling that this shop is one of the better and more interesting jewelers in Florence.

SILVERSMITH—FLORENCE

Giovanni Del Bono

Ponte Vecchio 2–4–6–8
Lungarno Acciaiuoli 1
Florence
Telephone: 275–502

Open daily except Sunday
10% discount
Medium to high

When Florentines shop for gifts of silver, they head for Del Bono. This long-time resident of the Ponte Vecchio offers a staggering assortment of handmade silverware in original and attractive designs. The shop's three floors, plain as they are, are filled to overflowing with merchandise.

You'll find silver platters in all shapes and and sizes—some so small they could hold little more than a wine bottle, others large enough to make an imposing display for your dining room. You'll see individual candleholders, multi-tiered candelabra, complete tea services, serving trays, decorative boxes, and cigarette containers. There's even a selection of antique silver.

The price range, you'll notice, is also varied. Some items are priced low enough to make them attractive "take-home" gifts. Other pieces are of the type that make special wedding or anniversary gifts which are destined to become family heirlooms.

We saw exquisite silver candelabra priced between $25 and $100, and if money is no object, there are candelabra priced up to $1000. Elegant silver tea services sell for $80 up to $800. Silver boxes, some with enamel inlay, make beautiful gifts and are priced between $25 and $85.

The Del Bonos, who have been making and selling their wares to Florentines ever since 1891, are one of the oldest silversmith firms in the city. Carlo Del Bono, the present owner, is the third generation to enter the business. He speaks with pride of his family's tradition, and strives to assure that its standards of quality and design continue to be maintained at a constant high level. He also attempts to offer good value for the price, realizing that he must do so to satisfy the discriminating Florentines.

We believe that he succeeds in both efforts admirably.

FINE TABLE LINENS—FLORENCE

Francesco Navone

Via della Vigna Nuova 2
(a few steps off Via Tournaboni)
Florence
Telephone: 20–909

Open daily except Sunday
10% discount
Expensive

Back at the turn of the century, J. P. Morgan, Andrew Mellon, Henry Frick, and Mrs. Jack Gardner shopped at Navone.

And even though it's now the 1970's, Signor Calligaris, the fifth generation of his family to operate this establishment, continues to treat his customers as his father and grandfather did, with dignity and deference.

The merchandise hasn't changed either. The same fine quality and workmanship that attracted American millionaires to Florentine linens 70-odd years ago continues to attract a well-to-do clientele now.

"Back in those days," says Signor Calligaris, "the rich Americans would buy our linens and laces by the kilometer. We also did a lot of business with the Russian nobility before the Revolution. Florence used to be a favored playground for royalty.

"That's all over now. Surprisingly, for the first time most of our customers are Italians. The Italians today have the financial means and they've always had the taste. They know and demand quality and that's what we offer them."

The quality is obviously the finest and the merchandise is priced accordingly. Any type of pattern can be made to order, and tablecloths may be ordered in varying lengths and sizes. We saw a superb set of place mats made of fine church linen with detailed shadow work and much embroidery. The price: $240 for a set of 8 napkins and 8 place mats.

We should quickly add that there are many items that sell for less, as well as many that sell for a good deal more. A set of fine linen place mats, with a border of hand embroidery that would grace any dining table, was selling for $80—for 8 napkins and 8 place mats. Some luncheon sets are as low as $30 per set of 8. These, too, are of pure linen, shot with silver and hand-edged.

"The point really is that no matter what the price, the quality remains constant. Therefore, for $20 or $30 we offer you fine material, but you can't expect loads of detailing," explains the Signor. "At that price we'd have to resort to machine embroidery, and we'd never do that!"

Naturally not. The Morgans, Mellons, Fricks, and Mrs. Jack Gardner would never approve.

TAF

Via Por. Maria 17R and 22R
Florence
Telephone: 23–190 and 296–037

Open daily except Sunday
10% discount
Medium

Tired of decorating your table in beige or white? TAF can add new sparkle to your dining room.

This light, bright, and cheerful shop has color everywhere, and the two floors at Number 17R are chock full of the delightful linen and embroidery for which Florence is noted.

TAF specializes in linens decorated with multicolored embroidery and colored linens decorated with contrasting embroidery. There are roses of every color and shading; there are daisys, petunias, and floral bouquets of every type and description—all lovingly appliquéed or embroidered onto linens. There are classical geometric designs also, and they take on a new life when embroidered with vibrant colored threads.

In addition to the large stock on hand at the shop, TAF makes tablecloths to order, and can match a favorite china pattern. In fact, they regularly work with architects and decorators to coordinate table linens with other furnishings in a home.

The firm has been in business since 1919. Today, seven members of the same family work together, each one supervising a workroom in which the products are designed and made, to insure continuing quality.

The prices? Quite reasonable. One place mat and matching napkin setting costs between $1.50 and $10. Tablecloths come in a wide range of prices, depending on size and workmanship. We saw several attractive round tablecloths with 8 matching napkins selling for between $20 and $30. Hand-embroidered bed linens also are available.

TAF sells lingerie as well, and the same loving care that goes into the linens appears on these personal articles. Slips, nightgowns, and undergarments are all hand-embroidered and delicately worked. Number 17R has the larger selection of linens, while Number 22R across the street specializes in the lingerie.

VALLI

Via Strozzi 4–6R
Florence
Telephone: 282–485

Open daily except Sunday
15% discount
Medium to medium high

Ladies who sew know that many of the most attractive fashion fabrics come from Italy. They also know that imported Italian fabrics tend, unfortunately, to be high in price.

If you're one of these nimble-fingered ladies, and you're going to visit Florence, by all means, stop off at Valli.

It's a large shop located in the center of town. Valli manufactures all the materials it sells, and because these materials are being sold in the country of origin, the prices are considerably more attractive than what you've been accustomed to.

There are rich-textured tweeds in both coarse and tight weaves, which are especially attractive for making up into suits. There are cottons, silks, and rich brocades, which come in the latest fashion colors and prints and make up especially well in dress patterns that reproduce couturier designs. Fabrics for evening dresses are a specialty here.

This is a busy shop. Although ready-to-wear has been introduced in Florence during the past few years, many Italians are still accustomed to having all their clothes sewn for them by a favored dressmaker or tailor. Valli has been serving the needs of such Florentines since 1930, and it's a popular local establishment.

Whether you have a favorite dressmaker of your own, or you're your own favorite dressmaker, an Italian fabric is sure to add an international flair to your wardrobe.

C. MOSCARDI

Via Tornabuoni 25R
Florence
Telephone: 24-414

Open daily except Sunday
10% discount
Medium high

When seventeenth-century Florentine nobility decorated their *palazzi*, they often turned to master woodcarvers for the finishing touches. The skills they valued so highly have not totally disappeared. Today, the Moscardi workroom is still turning out works of wood carved by hand in the style of the seventeenth century.

Moscardi is a rarity, for even in this city of artisans, there are few places which still maintain the old traditions of fine carving.

You enter the shop and see wood, wood, wood, in one form or another all around. On the street level of this narrow crowded shop the walls are covered with frames, the tables are filled with carved objects, and there are even works occupying the spaces under the tables. Upstairs you'll find more works in wood. All the objects are beautifully hand-crafted and the product of many hours of meticulous detailing.

Signor Visconti, the proprietor, tells us that most of his clientele are Italians who come from as far away as Milan and Rome. Many of them order custom designs. Others choose from the large selection of ready-made items available for purchase. We especially liked the frames for mirrors, which sold for between $80 and $320.

There also are picture frames, which we thought looked particularly attractive surrounding old prints; they're priced between $49 and $490. There are also lamp bases and a variety of wall hangings. The wood may be done in a natural color, stained, covered with gold leaf, or treated according to the customer's specifications.

Moscardi has been in business since 1894. If today's prices seem high, it's because Moscardi has refused to compromise with quality. It's an old-fashioned shop with old-fashioned standards, which we think is all to the good.

For the Collector: Art and Antiques

For the Collector: Art and Antiques

Rome is a city in which you'll find all sorts of little shops that are devoted to specialized collector items, a marvelous place in which to spend several mornings just browsing through elegant showrooms, musty storerooms, and outdoor stalls.

You'll come across rare books, medieval armor, old jewelry, Etruscan antiquities, ships in bottles, Roman and Greek coins. You'll find modern paintings and centuries-old prints. You may find a shop that deals in supernatural potions and you'll certainly find shops that deal in religious medallions.

A good way to start is by strolling the Via Babuino and the Via dei Coronari to see rare books, antiquities, art, and oddities.

If you're looking for religious objects such as scrolls, medals, paintings, and sculpture, go to Calbressa at Piazza Minerva 77.

If your taste runs to modern art, there's quite a bit to be seen in Rome (although Milan is the major center for contemporary art in Italy). There are several good galleries you might want to visit. Among them:

George Lester Gallery, Via Mario de'Firori 59A

Obelisco Gallery, Via Sistina 146

Odyssia Gallery, Via Liguria 36

Schneider Gallery, Rampa Mignanelli 10

These galleries carry expensive works of twentieth-century masters, including such internationally known Italian artists as Manzu, Morandi, and Marin. They also deal in the works of younger Italian painters who still sell at modest prices. Several dealers handle fine quality prints—etchings, lithographs, and woodcuts, which sell at prices starting as low as $30.

Rome also has numerous antique shops that deal in furniture. But local collectors tell us that unless you know exactly what you're doing, purchasing antique furniture can be a perilous task. Excellent copies and forgeries abound, and unless you have a skilled eye, it's almost impossible to know the difference.

By all means, however, visit the Roman flea market, held every Sunday morning in the Trastevere district at Porta Portese. It's open from 6 A.M. to 1 P.M., and you're liable to uncover anything from used household furniture to medals of Mussolini, from old Sicilian busts made of wood to a nineteenth-century urn or a rare antique. Whatever you find, the fun is in the looking. If you want to buy, be sure to bargain.

The city of Florence is a good place to purchase serious antique furniture. A sampling of antique shops in Florence can be quickly made by walking along the Via dei Fossi, Via Borgognissante, and Via Maggio.

If you purchase an antique, be sure to have the dealer give you a certificate of authenticity with a description of the piece you've acquired. It's essential to have this document if you are to get the piece out of Italy without difficulty and into the United States without duty. A duty-free piece, according to U.S. Customs, must be at least 100 years old.

Original works of art can be brought in duty-free with ease. But for this, too, you must have a certificate from the dealer, which describes your purchase as being an original.

FINE ART—ROME

LA MEDUSA

Via del Babuino 124
Rome
Telephone: 686–546

Open 9:30 A.M.–1 P.M. and 4:30–8 P.M. except Sunday and Monday morning
10% discount on international masters
20% discount on younger painters
Medium to high

La Medusa is a serious gallery which deals in works by twentieth-century European artists of international repute. It carries oils, sculptures, drawings, and prints in a wide range of prices. In addition, the gallery handles a number of what it considers to be promising young Italian painters, whose works sell at more modest prices. Yet these, too, are serious painters—you won't find any Roman versions of those mass-produced Paris street scenes here!

The works of Chagall, Picasso, Miro, Dubuffet, Braque, Klee, Tanguy, De Chirico, as well as the Cobra painters—Alechinsky, Appel, Jorn—all have been shown here in recent years. The English artists Butler, Moore, Chadwick, and Sutherland also have been exhibited. Works of contemporary Italian masters like Marino, Morandi, and the sculptor Manzu also are shown from time to time.

The gallery, located on the second and third floors of the building, is a quiet place with plenty of room to browse, to reflect, and to appreciate. The clientele includes international collectors and museum people as well as younger beginning collectors with more taste than money.

Signor Bruni himself is a collector, and he earnestly believes in the works he carries. His home is a showpiece for his own collection and is well known in the art circles of Rome.

If fine contemporary art is to your taste, La Medusa is well worth a visit.

OLD BOOKS AND PRINTS—ROME

LIBRERIA ANTIQUARIA QUERZOLA

Via del Babuino 153
Rome
Telephone: 679-0568

Open daily except Sunday
10% discount
Inexpensive to expensive

During the fifteenth century—in the early days of printing—the books that "sold" were those that had to do with the way to salvation. The works of theologians like St. Thomas Aquinas were what the reading public demanded.

Today, these early books are still selling, and they are in greater demand than ever—not for the purpose of soul-searching, but because these are rare collector's items.

You can still find a few such books for sale at Signora Querzole's, along with equally rare old prints. Signora Querzole is a member of the International Association of Antiquarian Book Dealers, and hers is known to be one of the best such establishments in Rome.

During our visit here, we looked through one fragile book, dated 1482, by St. Thomas Aquinas. We saw another yellowed book, dated 1494, written by Savonarola, the Dominican priest who opposed the rise of Humanism in Italy and was burned at the stake. One of the Signora's best finds is no longer in the shop. Established as the first book ever printed in Rome—date 1467—it was sent to the United States, to Yale University.

As for rare prints, we saw some beautiful eighteenth-century Venetian prints by Piranesi and Calaletto, and a treasure of a Tiepolo. These prints, which were relatively inexpensive just a few years ago, now are in great demand and cost thousands of dollars.

Of course the Signora has many less expensive items. The prints, in fact, start at $1, and there are a good many for under $50 and $100. We could not help thinking that some of these less expensive items would make handsome wall hangings—they mostly are topographic and geographic views of Italian cities.

The books, too, come in a variety of prices and conditions. Many are printed in Italian; some are in other languages.

The shop is a fascinating place to visit. It looks more like something out of the world of Charles Dickens than it does Old Rome. Whether you're a seasoned collector or a budding one, you'll find Querzole's well worth your time.

… ANTIQUE WEAPONS AND ARMOR—ROME

Aldo Soligo

Via del Babuino 161
Rome
Telephone: 673–910

Open 9:00 A.M.–1:00 P.M. and 3:30–8:15 P.M.
 except Sunday
15% or 20% discount, depending on item
Moderate to expensive

It stands there straight and tall (by medieval standards), a suit of tarnished armor that once adorned an Italian cavalier. Around it are helmets, swords, lances, and other paraphernalia from the days when battle was a gentleman's pastime. At Galleria Aldo Soligo, war has been relegated to its proper place—an historic oddity.

Soligo is the only place in Rome, perhaps in all Italy, where *armi antiche* (antique arms) are a specialty. Practically everything that has to do with war is crammed into this small shop.

You'll see an astonishing array of rifles, pistols, and antique blunderbusses priced from 35,000 lire (about $56) to 1,500,000 lire ($2420). Many date back to the days when Italy was still a collection of tiny and constantly warring states. But you'll also come upon Lugers and Mausers left behind when the Nazi armies fled Italy toward the end of World War II. So it's important to remember that United States gun-control laws require you to have a federal permit before bringing home any firearms that still shoot. (Otherwise, they'll be detained by Customs until you get the permit.)

But no permission is needed to bring home guns which *can't* be fired, or swords and armor. These—like the medals, uniforms, battle flags, insignia, military hats, and helmets which Soligo sells—make exciting decorations for a den or family room. What's more, you'll receive a guarantee of authenticity of anything you buy, and in the case of antiques you'll be given the proper credentials (again, for Customs, so they won't be subject to duty).

In addition to actual arms and militaria, Soligo has a fascinating assortment of prints, books, paintings, and other pieces dealing with war and warriors. You can even buy entire regiments of miniature soldiers fashioned from wood, china, metal, or paper-mâché.

Prices aren't low here, but your *Discovery* discount helps—to the tune of 15% off the tagged price on weapons, helmets, and armor, and 20% off the listed price of most other items. So if you're a collector, or you're looking for gifts that are both antique and unusual, don't overlook Soligo—a veritable arsenal of the past.

LORENZALE

Via del Babuino 165   Via Coronari 2–3
Rome   Rome
Telephone: 640-419   Telephone: 564-616

Open Monday to Saturday 9 A.M.–1 P.M. and
   3:30–7:30 P.M. (winter), 4:00–8:00 P.M. (summer)
15% discount
Expensive

Lorenzale specializes in model ships, but not the kind of model ships *we* used to build when we were youngsters playing with balsa and tissue paper. What Lorenzale sells are rarities, true objects of art.

Would you believe a miniature Dutch caravelle, dating from the eighteenth century, that is fashioned out of silver and priced at 3,500,000 lire? Well, believe it, because it's there — and 3,500,000 lire is $5645!

This, of course, is a high price. A companion piece to the caravalle, a Dutch galleon, costs only 300,000 lire—about $484 —but, then, it isn't silver. And there are other models that cost as little as 30,000 lire ($48). Some are even being made today, by artisans who work on commission from Lorenzale itself. But new or old, rare metal or common material, the workmanship is stupendous. The accuracy and attention to detail that go into these ships is awe-inspiring, especially when you realize that most of them could never even sail in a bathtub.

So what are they for? For collections. For people who, like us, built and played with model ships when they were kids, and now use more elaborate models as sculptures in their homes and offices. Not just Italians but foreigners, too, come to Lorenzale's small and crowded shops on Via del Barbuino and Via Coronari.

Nevertheless, you don't have to be a frustrated admiral to sail happily through Lorenzale. There are plenty of non-shipshape antiques here, including miniatures carved from jade and rare ivory pieces from China. There's also a very interesting selection of antique ceramic and porcelain objects, which are often more salable than sailable, because they're priced as low as 25,000 lire ($40).

What makes an antique unique is not just its age and craftsmanship but its rarity. We have seen very few as appealing as the unseaworthy charmers we found in Lorenzale's ship shops.

ANTIQUE FURNITURE—FLORENCE

GALLERIA LUIGI BELLINI

Lungarno Soderini 5
Florence
Telephone: 24-031

Open daily except Sunday
10% discount
Medium high to high

Bellini is for serious collectors. For this is one of the renowned antique dealers of Europe.

The firm began in 1876, when one Giuseppe Bellini obtained a license as an antiquarian. His son Luigi developed the business to new heights, helping to form many a great European collection and amassing a major collection of his own. Today, his sons Giuseppe and Mario carry on the family tradition.

To visit Bellini's is an experience. Housed in a fifteenth-century *palazzo* located on the banks of the Arno, this is probably the largest private antique dealer showroom in Europe. There are rooms upon rooms, leading into and out of one another in a labyrinth-like maze. And all that space is filled. The rooms contain a vast collection of Italian antiques—furniture and paintings —of all periods up to the eighteenth century. Many of the medieval and Renaissance pieces are exceedingly large, having been designed for the *palazzi* of the nobility, rather than the twentieth-century apartments of Florentine businessmen.

The quality of the pieces appears to be high. Bellini's peers agree, for Signor Giuseppe is president of the International Antique Dealers Association, as well as president of the Italian Antique Dealers Association.

The prices, of course, are in keeping with the importance of the pieces. They range from $100 to $200,000—and that's quite a range.

Some of the more important pieces in the gallery, as described by Signor Bellini, are a fourteenth-century wood sculpture representing Christ, two large figures of the sixteenth century attributed to Giovanni della Robbia, a fourteenth-century Sienese panel painted on gold with a figure of the Madonna and child, a bust by Donatello, believed to have been executed during the first half of the fifteenth century, and a view of the Grand Canal which Antonio Canaletto painted early in the eighteenth century.

There are smaller pieces as well, including the antique Italian earthenware called majolica.

If you wish to visit the gallery, it is requested that you call for an appointment first.

ANTIQUE DEALER—FLORENCE

CHESNE DAUPHINE

Lungarno Corsini 42R
Florence
Telephone: 283–401

Open daily except Sunday
10% discount
Inexpensive to expensive

Chesne Dauphiné is an antique dealer to antique dealers. Its prime business is finding choice pieces ao sell to other dealers. Retail sales to individuals constitute only a small part of the total volume.

"We prefer to work this way," explains the proprietor, "because other dealers know and can appreciate what we offer."

Therefore, as you might guess, the prices are favorable and the works are serious.

The business, in good Italian tradition, is run by father and son. Signor Chesne Dauphiné, the younger, speaks excellent English and is quite eloquent about the pieces he carries.

The gallery specializes in antiques of the Italian periods from 1300 to 1800. When we visited here, we found particularly attractive a set of Venetian painted chairs of the eighteenth century. We also liked the antique Italian ceramics—among the few smallish items that are shown.

Occasional English furniture also may be found. That's because many dealers are now seeking out Italian antiques in England and shipping them back home. In the process, a few English pieces accompany the shipment.

The turnover at Chesne Dauphiné is brisk, and the quality of merchandise on view is apt to vary considerably. If you visit just after a new shipment has arrived, you'll find lots of exciting pieces. At other times, the merchandise may be well picked over.

At any rate, if you like Italian antiques, it's worth dropping by. The gallery is well located, on the street that borders the Arno. The building is a seventeenth-century *palazzo* with vaulted ceilings. The atmosphere is comfortable and all the pieces are well displayed, so it's a pleasant place to browse. If you're looking for something specific, however, be sure to ask, because the Chesne Dauphinés have a second location at Via Lorenzo il Magnifico, 17R. It's in a more remote section of town, but it may hold just what you're looking for.

One thing we should note here. The prices on antiques—all over the world—tend to be fluid. We have negotiated a 10% discount for you, which applies to the initial quoted price. If you can do better on your own, we congratulate you. If you like to bargain, by all means try.

You Never Looked Better: Personal Care

You Never Looked Better: Personal Care

Having your hair done in Rome is like playing a part on center-stage. You innocently enter a barber shop or beauty salon and suddenly find that you're the supporting role in a great melodrama. Your hairdresser of course plays the lead part, and all sorts of bit players run on and off stage to keep the action lively. The stage set is the salon itself—sometimes subdued and underplayed, sometimes like something out of *La Dolce Vita*, but always the props are superbly placed for effect, and magnificent-looking machinery heightens the display.

By all means go and have your hair done in Rome. Better still, have a beauty treatment with it and let yourself be pampered from head to toe. If you've ever suffered from lack of attention, a Roman salon should more than make up for it.

Italian hairdressers, *parrucchieri*, rank among the best in the world. They learn their skills by apprenticing themselves to a leading salon at an early age, and they take their profession seriously, treating it as a creative art. You still see pink-cheeked adolescents learning their trade in the Roman salons today. They are the "extras" whose function often consists of looking, learning, and holding a hair dryer over your curls while the great man—the hairdresser—creates a marvelous look just for you.

Because they are so creative, the Italians have pioneered many of the revolutionary styles in the world of hair fashion. Remember the "Italian look" of a few years back? And of course you know the "teased look"—a noted Florentine hairdresser takes credit for introducing that to the United States, and its ramifications are still being felt today.

Italian beauty experts firmly believe that a woman looks only as good as she is made to feel. For this reason the Roman salon is more than a salon. It is a temple of beauty designed for effect, and the charm of the hairdresser should make you feel just as good as does the grooming itself. The theatrics and the pampering may appear a bit dramatic to an American observer, but ask any woman who's undergone the treatment. Be she American, German, English, or Italian, she'll love it.

Italian salons employ the latest equipment, and cosmetology is an integral part of the beauty business in Rome.

Cosmetology involves facials, massages, and special lotions and creams designed to restore or maintain a youthful appearance.

Does it work? Thousands of European women swear that it does, and it is a rapidly expanding field on this side of the ocean.

Such treatments can be expensive, depending on how much you want to have done. They can involve hours of labor and, sometimes, rather costly creams. So work out in advance what it is you want to try and determine what you will be paying for it.

A barber shop for men is no ordinary thing, either. Remember *The Barber of Seville?* Roman barbers have been trying to maintain that theatrical tradition ever since.

You ought not to walk into a *barberia* and ask for just a trim—that's like asking an artist to trace a picture done by someone else.

No! Genius must have an opportunity to express itself. The shape of your head must be analyzed and exclaimed upon. The razor must whisk this way and that. The scissors must snip and clip. The tonic must soothe and caress. Other barbers must come over and admire the work in progress. Finally the masterpiece is completed and everyone must show delight—yourself included.

Prices for haircuts, styling, manicures, pedicures, and the more conventional personal-care treatments run slightly less than what you would pay in a comparable top-flight beauty salon or barber shop back home. The prices we list are the base prices. (Your *Discovery* discount reduces them further.) Of course the neighborhood salon in Rome or Florence costs less than one that's located in a prime central location, and they are often quite good. But we frequently found that going to such places by taxi eats up whatever is saved in the rates. That's why we have not included any neighborhood places here.

Instead, the hairdressers and barbers we have selected are in the key locations in town, so most travelers will be able to reach them easily. The establishment you choose for yourself depends upon the sort of person you are and the mood you're in. There are many fine beauty salons and barbers in Rome and Florence. From the many, we have chosen a few—each different—but you can try any of them with confidence.

Some Helpful Phrases for Beauty Care

FOR WOMEN
Trim—*Taglio*
Shampoo—*Shampoo*
Set—*Messa in piega*
Manicure—*Manicure*
Comb-out—*Colpo di pettine*
Tinting—*Colorazione*
Color—*Colore*
Rinse—*Rifluesso*
Permanent—*Permanente*
Facial make-up—*Trucco*
Pedicure—*Callista*

FOR MEN
Wash and cut—
   Taglio dei capelli
Give me a shave—
   Mi fa la barba
Facial—*Messaggio*
Manicure—*Manicure*

BARBER SHOP
Piazza Manfredo Fanti 3
Rome
Telephone: 733–343

Open 8:00 A.M.–8:00 P.M. daily; closed Sunday afternoon and Monday
20% discount
Inexpensive

"What's the name of this barber shop?" we asked. The name? The name is "Barber Shop"! In Rome that's real class. The Italian word is *barberia,* but since most of the customers don't speak English, the translated words have a sophisticated ring.

At any rate, we liked "Barber Shop." It's a place where young Roman businessmen, actors, and workers go when they want fine styling and service at a moderate price.

The proprieter, Angelo Passeri, takes his work seriously, and gives each client the attention befitting a first-rate establishment. A routine haircut includes: a wash, a razor cut, air drying with a hand dryer, followed by a final trim with a scissor. The great work is finished off with a small bottle of aromatic Italian hair tonic which is poured over the head. (If you don't want this last touch, speak up fast.)

Angelo began learning the trade as a child and has been in the business since 1937. This new shop, located near the railway station, represents the realization of a dream, and is proof of his growing clientele. He's been at the present location for just two years, having previously had a smaller shop. Four barbers assist him now. The décor is pleasant and gay: a green tile floor, orange walls, and maroon chairs give a perky feeling that's appropriate for the youngish clientele. The place is busy, so it helps to make a reservation.

What we enjoyed most, though, was having a shave. What's so special about a shave? Well, with this shave, first your face is well prepared. Then it's massaged. Then it's shaved and cleaned. And just when you think you're finished, a huge Rube Goldberg-like contraption is wheeled over to you, plugged in and steam is blown over your face to make sure you're properly disinfected!

No English is spoken here, but with a few key phrases you'll manage nicely. Try *Mi fa la barba* for "Give me a shave," or *Taglio dei capelli* for "Give me a wash and cut."

The prices are modest. A haircut is $1.33. A wash is $1.00, and English tonic is $1.00. A shave is 85¢ and a facial is $2.00.

A good buy, and very Roman indeed!

MEN'S HAIRSTYLIST—ROME

Peppino

Via Mario de' Fiori 82
Rome
Telephone: 688–404

Open daily except Sunday, 8:30 A.M.–1:30 P.M. and 3:30–8:00 P.M.
10% discount
Medium

There's no question about it. This is one of the best *barbieri* in Rome. How good is he? Well, on the day we went there we found ourselves being shorn and styled and lathered alongside a member of Rome's nobility, a well-known Italian financier, and a would-be movie star.

What did all these gentlemen have in common? A simple conviction that Peppino is the best and most avant-garde barber in the city.

This establishment looks like a simple Italian barber shop, small and with just four barber chairs. But Peppino Ricciardo, the owner, is no ordinary barber. He is known all around town for his skill with a scissors. He was one of the first in Rome to master the long haircut for men, doing it in a way that makes it look respectable rather than juvenile. We have seen him take an unruly head of hair (our own) and transform it into the look of an Italian sophisticate (or so we'd like to believe).

Like many of Italy's master barbers, Peppino is a Sicilian—and proud of it! That, he tells us, is where the classic Italian barbers come from, after having served arduous and exacting apprenticeships. Pepppino has been in Rome for nearly 25 years now, and during that time has built up a faithful clientele. Several of his customers swear by him and will let no one else touch a hair of their head.

The prices are reasonable for all that talent: $2.30 for a haircut, 85¢ for a shave, and $3.35 for a facial massage that's memorable.

The shop is situated right in the heart of town, just a short walk from the Spanish Steps. As we said, the shop is small, so if you plan to go, Signor Peppino requests that you kindly call for an appointment first.

BEAUTY SALON—ROME

Spartaco e Ugo

Piazza Di Spagna 51 (2nd floor)
Rome
Telephone: 679–1802

Open 9:00 A.M.–8:00 P.M., daily except Sunday
10% discount
Medium high

An atmosphere of restrained confidence is what you feel upon entering this salon. And well you should, for Spartaco and Ugo have been serving Rome's more elegant women for many years. Their specialty is, simply, excellent service and a secure knowledge of how hair should be cut and styled.

The appearance of the shop is tasteful and subdued. The service is courteous and efficient. The personnel have been with the shop for many years and interact like one big happy family. Tony, the manicurist, who gives one of the best hand treatments in all Rome, has been here for 20 years. Paolo, a young hairdresser, has been here ever since he started plying his trade. Signor Spartaco himself has been at this location for 20 years, and was joined by Signor Ugo in 1954. Everyone knows what he is doing and does it well.

The clientele, who include glamorous movie stars, Roman high society, and, simply, women who care about their looks, all are made to feel equally at home here. While most of the clientele are Roman, English is spoken by both Signor Spartaco and some of the staff, so you too will be welcomed.

As one of the salon's clients explained it to us. "This is a place that isn't only fashionable now, but one that's always in fashion."

The prices: Shampoo and set—$3.55. Manicure—$2. Facial—$4. Make-up—$2.50. Pedicure—$4.85. A permanent—$14.50, and a touch-up, wash, and set—$9.70.

BEAUTY CARE AND SALON—ROME

femme Sistina

Via Sistina 75
Rome
Telephone: 640–260 or 683–451

Open 9:00 A.M.–8:00 P.M. daily except Sundays
La cortesia: A free eye make-up
Medium high

Femme Sistina is a fast-rising star in the world of beauty care. And small wonder! When you want to feel like a *duchessa* from head to toe, Femme Sistina will happily oblige. When you're weary and frazzled, they'll rejuvenate you. Whether you need a simple wash-and-set, facial and make-up, massage, or the whole works, your need will be skillfully met with an abundance of Italian know-how and charm.

The Femme Sistina team has a lot going for it. There are the two co-owners: Signor Rino Salomone is the expert in hair care and styling; Signora Lisette Lenzi is the specialist in cosmetology and beauty care (she has developed an excellent line of beauty products that go under the name of the shop). Both worked for many years at one of the leading Roman salons before going into business for themselves about 1961. Today, their staff includes a team of six hair stylists, each of whom has his own specialties, and several make-up and beauty-care experts.

The shop operates on the premise that women need—in addition to expert beauty treatment—a bit of pampering. "Soul balm," one of their loyal customers calls it. Whatever it is, it works, for the list of Italian and international clientele grows year by year.

Try the make-up and facial—they're costly, but marvelously satisfying. The way it's done here requires the effort of two girls working together. While one concentrates on the face and neck, the other creams and messages your arms and hands. As you lie wrapped in blankets with your feet resting high, take in the delicious aromas. Rose milk or almond milk cleanses your face, a mentholated mask refreshes it. The make-up that follows will bring forth a glow you never knew you had. The reflection that looks back at you in the mirror is much more glamorous than you remembered.

Now you're ready for that chance encounter with Marcello Mastroianni.

Some prices: $4 for a pedicure; $4 for a wash and set (including a free comb-out the following day); $1.60 for a manicure; and $7 for a facial including make-up. A separate eye make-up, usually $1.60, is complimentary with your *Discovery* Card when you purchase some other service of the salon.

BEAUTY SALON—ROME

"Filippo"

Via Condotti 91
Rome
Telephone: 671–498 or 674–907

Open 9:00 A.M.–8:00 P.M., every day except Sunday
10% discount
Expensive

Want to be fussed over in a modernistic salon with banks of mirrors, black ceilings, and futuristic hair dryers that come at you from out of the walls? Want to be surrounded by sophisticated Italians, jet-setters, and theatrical people while your looks are being refurbished?

That's what happens at Filippo's.

It's a swinging place to go, a place to see and to be seen. But don't let the atmosphere fool you into thinking that's all there is. For the truth is that Filippo has made his reputation among beauty-conscious Romans by being good—very good. His hairdos are sophisticated and stylish. His personnel are well-trained and know their business. The service is fast and efficient. Filippo himself is noted for the excellent haircuts he gives. If you want to come home looking like a Roman pace-setter, Filippo can "do" you beautifully. Customers here are primarily Italian and European, but enough English is spoken so that you'll have no problem.

Filippo has just opened a salon for gentlemen around the corner at Via della Carrozze 55, with the prices for a haircut about the same as for women. (The *Discovery* discount applies there as well.)

The prices for beauty care at Filippo's are on the high side. Wash and set—$4. Haircut—$6. By Filippo himself—$10. Facial—$5.70. Make-up—$3.10. Pedicure—$5. Permanent—$18. A manicure—$2.

The salon also has a boutique where Italian, French, and English knitwear, coats, belts, and gift items are sold. A nice place to browse.

TROTTA WIGS

Via Lazio 9 and Via Frattina 99
Rome
Telephone: 484-786

Open 9:00 A.M.–7:30 P.M., daily except Sunday
10% discount
Medium

If you want to be a new you, why not try a wig or two? Trotta, Rome's leading wigmaker, has been selling his wares to fashionable Italians for several years now.

As you probably know, many of the better wigs sold abroad are imported from Italy. Here in Rome you can buy them at the source.

There are eight Trotta Wig shops in Rome, with two that are conveniently located for travelers. The Via Lazio location is right around the corner from the Via Veneto, in a private building one flight up (be sure to take the staircase on your right). The Via Frattina location is also one flight up (on what Romans call the first floor).

Each salon also has a special room for men who may wish to buy a hairpiece in privacy. Men's wigs, by the way, are a small but growing part of the business.

See Riccardo, the director on Via Lazio, or Elia, the director on Via Frattina.

What makes the Trotta organization so good? For one thing, the firm goes through the entire process of creating a wig—from buying the hair to making the wig to styling it. All Trotta wigs are guaranteed 100% Italian hair. And each shop has its own stylists who create up-to-date wigs, wiglets, and falls, both casual and elegant.

Prices are a bargain by American standards. A wiglet of human hair goes for as little as $20. A fall costs from $60 to $90, with the more expensive one being a long full piece. A short-cut wig sells for as little as $40, a full wig can run up to $130, and there's a large selection in between.

We saw an elaborate wig that had been done up for a formal evening occasion with lots of long curls that cost the buyer $84. The eight to ten basic styles come made up in a variety of sets and colors. If you are lucky enough to find your color ready, a set can be done for you in a matter of hours. If your color has to be specially prepared, that wig can be finished and rushed to you within two days.

BEAUTY SALON—FLORENCE

Dante G.

Lungarno Corsini 36R
Florence
Telephone: 294–893

Open: 9:00 A.M.–7:30 P.M., daily except Sunday
10% discount
Medium

Dante likes Americans and they return the compliment.

The Florentines like him, too, for he's one of the best hairdressers in the city.

Signor Dante's love affair with Americans stems from his two trips to the United States in 1955 and 1956. On those occasions, after having introduced Italian hair styles to U.S. audiences, he was awarded the "Golden Caesar" and the "Golden Oscar" by a leading Boston department store. Dante also won renown by being one of the creators of hair-teasing.

Signor Dante is a member of one of those Florentine families which date back to the thirteenth century, so both his name and his reputation are respected by the local citizenry. His shop by the banks of the Arno River is small, but it's busy all day long.

This charming Italian gentleman has some very definite opinions about how women should look, and he applies these attitudes to his work. He explains, "I believe in grooming women to please men. Women should look like women, not like a great confusion."

Contrary to some present trends, Dante adds: "I believe in a look with balance. Long hair looks best with short skirts, and short hair looks best with long skirts. The maxi-look combined with long hair just doesn't work."

Dante is a member of Intercoiffure, an international association of select hairdressers located around the world, and travels regularly to meetings abroad in order to keep abreast of the latest in hair fashion trends. His specialty is cutting and styling hair. His clientele are a cosmopolitan mix, well-to-do for the most part.

The prices at Dante's are on a par with the better salons in Florence. (They run slightly below comparable prices in Rome.) A wash and set costs about $3.50. A manicure costs $1.30.

Rome After Dark: Nightclubs

Rome After Dark

Why "Rome After Dark"? Why not "Rome *and Florence* After Dark"? Because, as an American friend of ours living in Florence told us, "There's practically nothing at all in Florence after dark. They go out to eat at 7:30 or 8, and then they roll up the sidewalks at 11 o'clock." Night life isn't the Florentine style.

Rome is different. Rome is more alive. Rome moves, sometimes all night long. The clubs are crowded, the coffee bars are bustling, the girls in their little Fiat cars are cruising around looking for customers.

Yet even at its best, the night life of Rome is a far cry from London, Paris, or New York. Only within recent years has there been enough prosperity to support clubs and discotheques. Only within recent years have moral restrictions against sensual pleasures—even the more innocent sensual pleasures—been loosened. Rome has a lot of catching up to do.

But it's trying.

Dance clubs, both discotheques and clubs featuring live orchestras, proliferate throughout the city. Some are large and opulent, with brilliant décor and lighting effects, while others are small and intimate. In most, the music is vibrant, contemporary "rock," and American and English musicians are much in vogue.

Of nightclubs with elaborate floor shows, which abound in London and Paris, Rome has practically none—just a few places which cater almost strictly to tourists. The habit of spending tens of thousands of lire to watch a kick-line is one which the average Roman has not yet acquired.

Instead, Roman night life tends to focus on the coffee bars which are everywhere throughout the city. As in discotheques and cocktail lounges, coffee-bar action hits its stride about 11 in the evening and continues unabated until the wee hours of the morning.

Less frenetic but thoroughly enjoyable—if you're a music-lover—are the operas, held during the winter at the opera house on Via del Viminale and during the summer under the stars in the Baths of Caracalla. The world-famous Academy of St. Cecilia, too, holds summer concerts outside, at the Basilica of Maxentius.

Also popular during the summer months are "Sound and Light" shows at the Forum. These spectacles, in which the ruins themselves are the actors, use music, narration (in English), and colored lights so brilliantly that it's easy to believe yourself in ancient Rome. "Sound and Light" is something you shouldn't miss.

Night life in Rome may not be quite as varied as in London or Paris, but there's certainly more than enough to keep you entertained.

CLUB GATTOPARDO

Via Mario de' Fiori 97
Rome
Telephone: 684-838

Open every night from 10:00 P.M. on
La cortesia: Second drink is on the house
Moderate

The music drives and pounds and the strobe lights flash and flicker while sophisticated Romans dance and drink all night long at Club Gattopardo—one of the most beautiful nightclubs in Europe.

It all adds up to a vastly entertaining evening.

Gattopardo looks like something right out of a movie set. Feels like it, too. Continuous music, both rock and conventional, is played by two alternating groups. The dance floor is spacious, and the lighting plays on it constantly, now illuminating, now concealing. The dancers take on the air of something mysterious —like a Fellini movie come to life.

When you're not dancing, you sit things out on contemporary Italian furniture surrounding the dance floor—couches covered in rich gray velvet and so soft that once you sink into them, only the driving music makes you want to get up again. This is no little nightspot where everyone huddles together. Seating faces in all directions, so you have plenty of privacy.

Yet it's all very reasonable. The price of admission is the price of the first drink, $3.20. Each successive drink costs $2.00 and you're welcome to stay all evening. Snacks and late supper specialties, including pizza, also are available.

Giuseppe Coppola is the proprietor. Unlike most nightclubs in Rome, which grew out of restaurants, his was planned from the start to be a supper club, and is well done. Signor Coppola hovers around the club most evenings, making sure that everything is just so. The bands that play here are among the best in France and Italy. A new group is brought in each month, so that the atmosphere never grows stale, and the beat never winds down. Only the rock-playing organist—yes, rock-playing organist—who fills in between sets is a permanent fixture.

The clientele are mostly Romans of varying ages, many youngish, all smartly (or at least interestingly) dressed. If you're alone and just want to watch the action, you can sit at the bar—but there are no pickups here. Saturday night is jammed, so if you can, try another evening. The action starts at about 10:30 and builds up from there on. The club is well-located, just a few steps from the Piazza Di Spagna, and is worth visiting whether you're a dancer or simply a looker-on.

DISCOTHEQUE—ROME

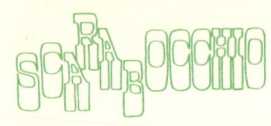

Piazza dei Ponziani 8C, Trastevere
Rome
Telephone: 500–495 (reservations needed)

Open nightly from 10 P.M.–4 A.M.
La cortesia: Reduced price on all drinks after the first
Moderate

You may recognize Lo Scarabocchio, even though you've never been there before. It's one of the places frequently used for filming nightclub scenes in Italian movies.

The reason is obvious. Lo Scarabocchio is stunning. Walls covered with red, gold, and blue velvet, candles lit on the tables, lusciously comfortable sofas and easy chairs to sink into, and brilliant psychedelic light-effects playing on the walls. And as if all that weren't enough, the dance floor is illuminated from *below,* to create the effect of dancing almost in the dark.

But you don't dance to live music. This is strictly a discotheque, with stereophonic music coming at you from every direction. As it happens, it's very good music, lively and up-to-date, the kind of music currently popular with Lo Scarabocchio's habitués, who are chiefly Roman society and movie people. Their constant presence not only spells financial success for owner Gianni Orlando but creates a situation where everyone seems to know everyone else. That shouldn't prevent you from going, however, No one really cares who knows whom so long as everyone has a good time. Which means that if you're not inhibited by celebrities, they won't be inhibited by you.

There's no entrance fee or cover charge, so drinks at Lo Scarabocchio are slightly expensive—2000 lire (about $3.25) at a table and 1000 lire at the bar. But your *Discovery cortesia* will reduce the price for every drink after the first to 1000 lire at the table, 700 lire (about $1.10) at the bar.

Unlike many discotheques and nightspots, Lo Scarabocchio doesn't feel the need to advertise itself, and has actually carried this modesty to the point of not bothering to put its name outside. So look for the number 8C and a red lamp on the side of the building.

Just make sure you phone for reservations before you come. Lo Scarabocchio only has room for 160 guests, and its "regulars" use it almost like a private club, so it's likely to be crowded. Once you're on the inside, however, you're really in.

NIGHTCLUB—ROME

Piper Club

Via Tagliamento 9
Rome
Telephone: 854-459

Open nightly 10:00 A.M.-3:00 A.M. (also 4–8 P.M. Thursday, Saturday, and Sunday)
La cortesia: Second drink on the house
Moderate

Say anything you have to say before entering the Piper. Once you're down in this enormous cellar, no one can hear a word. For Piper is one of the wildest, noisiest, most uninhibited clubs in Europe, so much so that it's actually difficult to hear yourself think, let alone talk. On any given evening, upwards of 800 people pack into this glossy, flossy nightspot to rock enthusiastically to the sounds of two driving beats, one from a big Italian orchestra and one from an imported English or American group.

In a way, it's fantastic—a fury of frenzied sound from 85 huge loud-speakers and a flashing of psychedelic colors from 350 spotlights. The clientele are pretty fantastic, too—long-haired youngsters and gyrating would-be youngsters who fling themselves around with reckless abandon. As a young European newspaperman with us put it, in an allusion we're still trying to unravel, "It's crazy." But crazy *wild* or crazy *nuts?* He didn't say. You'll have to decide that for yourself.

We had the notion, however, that some people were already deciding. Amid all the terrific enthusiasm up on the bandstand and out on the dance floor, a number of very serious-looking older people simply sat on the sidelines and stared. No dancing. No involuntary finger-drumming or foot-tapping. Just staring. As if they were trying to analyze the psychology that makes people swing as wildly as the Piper's "regulars" do. It was strange and incongruous—most people trying to dance themselves into a state of ecstasy, and a handful trying to figure out why!

Prices at the Piper are somewhat high—entrance fee and first drink come to 2000 lire, about $3.25, with subsequent drinks priced at 1500 lire, about $2.45. But with your *Discovery* Card, the second drink is complimentary.

Despite the heat and noise generated by the music and dancing, the club remains comfortable, because it's completely air-conditioned—something that not many European clubs can say for themselves. And the atmosphere really makes a wild scene. Obviously, Piper isn't for everyone. But if you're young, and in a holiday mood, you might well find it irresistible.

NIGHTCLUB—ROME

LE COQ D'OR

Via Flaminia Vecchia 493
Rome
Telephone: 393-247

Open nightly 10:00 P.M.–3:00 A.M.
La cortesia: Second drink on the house
Moderate

Sharing a fifteenth-century villa with the restaurant Le Coq d'Or is a lively, popular nightclub of the same name. So if you come for dinner and fall under the spell of one of Rome's most spectacular settings, the obvious thing is to continue the evening in the nightclub.

On the other hand, you might just have dinner elsewhere and come in later for drinks and dancing. The view is the same as the restaurant's and the atmosphere is equally sophisticated and pleasant.

Le Coq d'Or nightclub consists of five rooms furnished only with tables and comfortable sofas. A quartet plays the latest Italian hits with typical Latin exuberance—no old-fashioned slow stuff or outmoded South American rhythms but a driving move-move-move sort of music that lets you fully express yourself out on the dance floor.

Not that this means the junior jet-setters have taken over. Far from it. Le Coq d'Or appeals more to well-dressed, well-groomed types who, though mainly under 40, regard nightclubbing as entertainment rather than a way of life. People come with mates or dates, not to meet or mingle.

The first drink here costs 2000 lire (about $3.25) and additional drinks are priced at 1000 lire. With your *Discovery* Card, however, *la cortesia* will be your second drink on the house. (You pay for the first one.) Just about anything you want is available—from whiskey to cognac to Irish coffee to cocktails.

If you come in late and you're hungry, don't hesitate about ordering food. Though the menu is confined to specialty dishes —spaghetti, crepes suzette, and the like—they come from the same kitchen as the restaurant food and are thoroughly delicious.

Rome, as it won't take you long to discover, is a city filled with nightspots—some sleazy, most legitimate, but all doing a thriving business. Only a few, however, can for one reason or another honestly be classed as elegant. Le Coq d'Or, in its centuries-old villa by the Tiber, is one of the few.

Looking Around and Getting Around

Looking Around and Getting Around

Tales of Roman traffic jams have spread around the world. Stories of the difficulties people have in finding their way around the city are commonplace. But Rome has been much maligned. It is actually a relatively comfortable city in which to be a stranger.

A few simple facts will make everything clear.

The first thing to do in Rome is pick up a *detailed* map of the city, detailed because many of the most interesting sights are tucked away on side streets away from the broad avenues. Good maps are on sale at most bookshops, newsstands, and hotels. Then orient yourself on two places—your hotel, of course, and the Piazza Venezia, which Romans themselves use as a reference point.

If you'd like to rent a car, go ahead. Except during peak rush periods, traffic isn't nearly as bad as legend makes it seem. Especially during the evening hours, and away from the center of the city, driving is not much more difficult in Rome than anywhere else, and it certainly helps you to learn your way around.

In Florence, matters are even simpler. Practically everything is within walking distance, anyway.

Whether in Rome or Florence, however, taxis are inexpensive and easy to get. They don't cruise around looking to be hailed, as they do in London, Paris, and New York, but line up before taxi stands in the piazzas waiting for fares. If you speak a little Italian, you can also phone 117 and a cab will be sent directly to you.

Taxi rates are low. In Rome: 190 lire (31¢) for the first 220 meters or two minutes, and 20 lire (3¢) for additional 220 meters or two minutes. Passengers in excess of two cost 50 lire (8¢) per person. Night rates are slightly higher—between 10 P.M. and 7 A.M., the driver is permitted to add 150 lire (24¢) to whatever appears on the meter. Trunks or suitcases are carried for 100 lire (16¢) each.

Florence taxis charge 140 lire (22¢) for the first 500 meters (about ⅓ mile) or eight minutes, 30 lire (4¢) for every 250 meters or two minutes thereafter. Between 9 P.M. and 6 A.M. there's a 50-lire surcharge. Suitcases cost 30–100 lire each, depending on the site.

Once you're settled in your hotel, however, you might tackle the public transportation. Both Rome and Florence are served by streetcars and buses, and cost from 20 to 50 lire (3¢–8¢) per person in Rome, 40 lire (7¢) in Florence. Real bargains. All entrances are at the rear, all exits at the front. A bus stop is called a *fermata*, and at each there is a sign listing the route numbers of all buses which stop there. To make things easy, spend a few lire on the official, multilingual A.T.A.C. bus map of Rome, which clearly indicates all different routes. It's available at newsstands.

For an around-the-city bus trip, take the *Circolare Destra* (CD) bus 21 or the *Circolare Sinistra* (CS) bus 20 from the Porta Pinciana, at the end of the Via Veneto. They go in opposite directions yet follow the same route, so whichever one you take, you'll wind up back where you started.

There is also a subway, called *Metropolitana*, which travels only from the main railroad station to EUR, the satellite city which Mussolini planned for Rome's southern suburbs. EUR has never been completed, although what has been built is certainly impressive and worth seeing.

Many of Italy's museums are free, while others charge only a modest admission fee. But you may, for 500 lire, buy a pass, called the *Italia Nostra* card, which admits you to all state-owned museums, ruins, and gardens in the country without further payment. It's available in the United States and Canada at offices of the Italian Tourist Bureau, and costs 95¢.

Finally, we would like to recommend that you buy two special books when you get to Italy. Though printed in English, they're not sold in the United States or Canada, which is unfortunate, because you should have time to read them leisurely. In Rome, buy the small, leather-bound *Rome Past and Present: A Guide to the Monumental Centre of Ancient Rome with Reconstructions of the Monuments,* a brilliantly illustrated booklet with full-color photographs of the ruins and celluloid overlays depicting artist renderings of these same ruins as they looked in their prime. Price: 3500 lire (about $5.65) and worth every lira. In Florence, buy *Florence: An Appreciation of Her Beauty,* by Piero Bargellini, former mayor of the city. It contains the best and most complete description of Florence's museums, churches, monuments, and gardens that we have ever seen. Price: 1200 lire (about $1.95).

And if at the end you get stuck for information or directions, you can always turn to the concierge at your hotel. His help can prove invaluable to you in looking around and getting around.

APPIAN LINE

Via Vittorio Veneto 171
Rome
Telephone: 474–511

Open daily
20% discount on tours booked directly with the company
Standard

If your time in Rome is limited, or you want a quick survey of the sights before deciding where to concentrate your attention, a guided tour might well be the way to begin your visit.

The Appian Line, the largest touring company in Italy, can show you Rome, and practically everything from Florence to Capri, in the comfort of deluxe motor coaches with multi-language guides. In order to receive your 20% discount, go directly to the office at 171 Via Veneto or phone the firm personally—don't reserve through your hotel. Your *Discovery* Card and discount cover one family unit—two adults related by blood or marriage, and the children with them. A sampling of the tours:

Tour		Departures	Rates per Person
1.	Piazza Venezia, Imperial Forum, Colosseum, Circus Maximus, St. Paul Outside the Walls.	*Morning*	2000 lire (about $3.25)
2.	Fountain of Trevi, Panthéon, Basilica of St. Peter in the Vatican, Spanish Steps, View of Rome from Janiculum Hill, Castel St. Angelo, Trastevere.	*Afternoons*	2000 lire (about $3.25)
3.	Villa Borghese, Quarter of the Foreign Academies, Vatican Museum, Sistine Chapel.	*Morning: except Sundays & holidays*	2000 lire (about $3.25)
4.	Basilica of Santa Maria Maggiore, Church of St. Peter in Chains and Michelangelo's statue of Moses, Holy Stairs, ancient Appian Way, Catacombs, Baths of Caracalla.	*Afternoons*	2000 lire (about $3.25)
5.	Tivoli, Villa d'Este, Hadrian's Villa	*Afternoons*	2800 lire (about $4.60)
6.	Castelgandolfo and wine-producing "Castelli Romani" region.	*Afternoons*	2100 lire (about $3.40)

Tour		Departures	Rates per Person
23.	One-day excursion to Monte Cassino, Capri, Sorrento, including lunch, dinner, fees. Return to Rome about 11 P.M.	April 1– September 30	15,000 lire (about $24.20)
31.	Two-day excursion to Naples, Pompeii, Sorrento, Capri. Includes meals, entrance fees, hotel (at Sorrento). Return to Rome at 11 P.M. of 2nd day.	All year round	25,000 lire (about $40.80)
41.	Three-day excursion to Naples, Pompeii, Sorrento, Capri, Positano, Amalfi, and Ravello. Includes meals, entrance fees, hotel (at Sorrento). Return to Rome at 11 P.M. of 3rd day.	All year round	35,000 lire (about $56.45)

Timetable for daily departures of tours 1 through 6: In summer, April 1 to September 30—departures from major hotels begin at 8 A.M. and 2:30 P.M.; from the company office at Via Veneto 171 at 8:30 A.M. and 3 P.M. In winter, October 1 to March 31—departures from the major hotels begin at 8:30 A.M. and 2 P.M.; from Via Veneto 171 at 9 A.M. and 2:30 P.M.

Timetable for departures of excursions 23, 31, and 41: Hotel departures begin at 6:45 A.M.; from Via Veneto 171 at 7:15 A.M.

All rates quoted are those *before* your 20% discount.

CAR RENTAL—ROME

euro self drive

Via Sicilia 7–13
Rome
Telephone: 460–355 or 474–471

Fiumicino Airport
Rome
Telephone: 601–879

Open 24 hours a day
10% discount on fixed rates (see below)
Standard

Exciting as Rome is, fascinating as Florence is, there's an Italy out beyond their city limits that no visitor with extra time should miss. As with the United States and Canada, the best way to see Italy is by car. Not only do you learn your way around but you see what you want when you want to, following no one's schedule but your own. So unless you've already reserved a drive-yourself-car through your travel agent back home, you might consider contracting Euroselfdrive, which has been helping visitors help themselves in Italy ever since 1920.

Euroselfdrive's cars are mostly Fiats (Cadillacs and Mercedes are sometimes available for chauffeur-driven tours), and the firm maintains a network of garages throughout Italy where parking and service are available free. Motor oil and normal maintenance are free, too (just turn in your receipt for a refund), but fixed rates do not include gasoline, and government taxes are extra. You're responsible for all traffic violations, of course.

Within that framework, and subject to change, naturally, here are the Euroselfdrive rates:

Type of Car	Number of Seats	Price per Day	Price per Week	Charge per Kilometer
Fiat 500 Luxe	2	1700 lire/$ 2.80	10,000 lire/$16.20	29 lire/4.7¢
Fiat 850 Sp.	4	2600 lire/$ 4.20	15,000 lire/$24.20	38 lire/6.2¢
Fiat 128	4	3000 lire/$ 4.90	18,000 lire/$29.10	45 lire/7.3¢
Fiat 124	4	3400 lire/$ 5.50	20,000 lire/$32.30	49 lire/8¢
Fiat 125 Sp.	4	3800 lire/$ 6.20	23,000 lire/$37.10	58 lire/9.4¢
Fiat 2300 (manual or automatic)	5–6	6500 lire/$10.50	40,000 lire/$64.50	69 lire/11.2¢
Fiat 124 Spider	2	6500 lire/$10.50	40,000 lire/$64.50	69 lire/11.2¢
Volkswagen Minibus	8	6500 lire/$10.50	40,000 lire/$64.50	69 lire/11.2¢

Extra charges: Insurance is $1.50 per day, $7.50 per week if you want it. And you absolutely *do* want it—even if you have a million-dollar policy back home! A safety belt is another $3 per week. Radio? That's 50¢ a day.

If you're planning to drive yourself in Italy (or anywhere in Europe, for that matter), make sure you bring your operator's permit with you. And an International Driver's License, available through your local travel agent or automobile association, is $3 well spent. Have a safe trip!

EYRE & HUMBERT

Piazza Rucellai 4–7
Florence
Telephone: 275–611 and 294–527

Open 9 A.M.–1 P.M. and 3–7 P.M. Monday to Friday, 9 A.M–1 P.M. Saturday
10% discount
Standard

Mr. Eyre was American. Monsieur Humbert was Swiss. Together, they opened a travel service in Florence in 1881. In the years since then, it has grown into one of the largest and most respected guide services in Italy. Competent and multilingual, Eyre & Humbert operates private tours with car and driver-guide, and deluxe motor-coach tours of Florence and the surrounding areas.

Tour	Operation	From	Person
1. Half-day tour of Medici Chapel, with Michelangelo masterpieces (visit). St. Lawrence's Church, Duomo, Baptistery, Campanile, Viale dei Colli, Piazzale Michelangelo for panoramic view of the city, Pitti Palace (visit), and Boboli Gardens. Departs 9–9:15 A.M. Returns about 12:30 P.M. (On Tuesdays, Accademia is substituted for Pitti.)	All year round, for private and motor-coach services.	Major hotels	2500 lire (about $4)
2. Half-day tour of Piazza della Signoria, Loggia dei Lanzi with Cellini's Perseur, Neptune Fountain, Uffizi Gallery (visit), Piazza SS Annunziata, Fiesole (Etruscan town overlooking Florence and Arno Valley) with short stop, and Church of Santa Croce. Departs 2–2:15 P.M., returns about 6 P.M. (On Mondays, Bargello will be substituted for Uffizi.)	All year round for private and motor-coach services.	Major hotels	2500 lire (about $4)
3. Morning tour to Cascine Park, Lungarno Vespucci, Lungarno Corsini, Via Tornabuoni, Duomo, Via del Proconsole, Bargello (National Museum: visit), Liazza dei Giudici, Lungarni, Piazza Beccaria, Piazza della Liberti, Accademia (visit). Departs 9–9:15 A.M., returns about 12:30 P.M.	Private service all year round, motor-coach April 1–October 31. Daily except Monday and Tuesday.	Major hotels	2500 lire (about $4)
4. "Arts & Crafts Tour" covers laboratories and factories of Florence. Half-day laboratory tour covers establishments manufacturing leather articles, gold and silverwares, straw products, and ceramics. Full-day tour includes above plus one of the following factories: bronze foundry, School of Florentine Mosaic, *Chianti* wine cellar. In each instance, you learn the historical background and observe the entire manufacturing or creative process.	Private service all year round.	Your hotel	Half day: 12,500 lire (about $20.16) Full day: 17,500 lire (about $28.28)

*Prices listed are the basic rates, *before* your 10% *Discovery* discount.

Tour	Dates of Operation	Departs From	Rates per Person*
5. Afternoon excursion to Pisa, about 60 miles from Florence, takes you over lovely Tuscan countryside to visit the famous Leaning Tower, cathedral, Baptistery, and other landmarks in this ancient university town on the banks of the Arno. Departs 1:30–2:00 P.M., returns about 6:30 P.M.	Motor-coach service April 1–October 31, private service all year round.	Major hotels	3400 lire (about $5.48)
6. Full-day excursion to Siena and San Gimignano travels past vine-covered hills and olive groves to view Siena's medieval architecture and art masterpieces. After lunch, tour continues to many-towered San Gimignano, preserved nearly intact since the Middle Ages. Depart 8:30 A.M., Return about 7 P.M.	Motor-coach service March 15–October 31. Private service all year round.	Major hotels	Without lunch: 3500 lire (about $5.65) With lunch: 5200 lire (about $8.39)
7. Half-day visit to Tuscan villas and gardens covers a slightly different itinerary each day. Among the areas covered are Forte di Belvedere, Boboli Gardens, and Villa i Tatti.	Motor-coach service only. April 1–June 30.	Piazza Strozzi	2500 lire (about $4)

*Prices listed are the basic rates, *before* your 10% *Discovery* discount.

Finding a Good Hotel

Finding a Good Hotel

Not all hotels in Italy are called hotels. Some are called *albèrgo*, which is Italian for hotel. The two words mean the same thing, although as a general rule, the more elegant hotels prefer the non-Italian term.

There are, in Rome, hundreds of hotels of virtually every type and description. Some, in the deluxe category, are on a par with the most luxurious hotels anywhere in the world. First-class hotels, too, are usually very good, and second-class hotels are often quite comfortable. By the time one reaches down to the third-class hostelries, however, quality begins to wear a bit thin, and we would strongly urge you to stay out of fourth-class hotels altogether—unless you're accustomed to roughing it. (Categories, by the way, are not based on our judgments; these rankings are official, determined by the Italian government.)

In selecting these Roman and Florentine hotels, we have chosen *albèrgi* which, in the judgment of our Roman and Florentine associates and ourselves, are particularly attractive and well-run. But hotels, like restaurants and shops, can change management, rates, attitudes, and policies. All are well-recommended, however, at the time of writing.

Here, then, are prices—for double room with bath:
Deluxe—8060–18,600 lire ($13.00–$30.00)
1st Class—5580–12,400 lire ($9.00–$20.00)
2nd Class—3400–6820 lire ($5.50–$11.00)

These, incidentally, are high-season rates—May 15 to October 31. Off-season rates may be a bit lower.

What's more, deluxe hotels in Rome and Florence add a service charge of 18% and a general tax of 3%. Service charges in lower ranked hotels are correspondingly lower, and the general tax is only 1%. There are, however, additional charges such as the daily sojourn tax, and restaurant and bar taxes.

Regardless of which category you choose, consult a travel agent before making your reservation. His job is to know the quality and availability of accommodations, and to advise you on current rates as well as facilities. We mention the following hotels only in the event that you arrive in Rome or Florence with no place to stay, grow disenchanted with where you're booked, or prefer to make your reservations direct:

Hotels in Rome

Deluxe

Hassler Villa Medici
Piazza Trinità de'Monte 8, Rome
Telephone: 682–651
> This distinguished European-style hotel, beautifully situated at the top of the Spanish Steps, offers modern conveniences and fine service. Considered to be one of the best hotels in Rome. 120 rooms.

Excelsior
Via Vittorio Veneto 125, Rome
Telephone: 489–031
> Situated on the famed Via Veneto, this big bustling hotel is popular with Americans. Air-conditioning and all the amenities. 400 rooms.

Cavalieri Hilton
Via Cadlolo—Monte Mario, Rome
Telephone: 3151
> Located near St. Peter's and surrounded by 15 acres of woodland park. Features a swimming pool and tennis courts. A bit out of the central area. 400 rooms.

Parco dei Principi
Via G. Frescobaldi, Rome
Telephone: 841–071
> This modern hotel offers rooms with balconies that overlook the lovely Borghese Gardens. It also has its own private park with swimming pool. 210 rooms.

First-class

Raphael
Largo Febo 2, Rome
Telephone: 656–9051
> This small hotel offers attractive deluxe accommodations at lower than deluxe rates. Situated next to the Piazza Navonna, a quiet but central location. 190 rooms.

De la Ville
Via Sistina 69, Rome
Telephone: 688–941
> This well-situated hotel, located near the Spanish Steps and central to shopping, has recently been redecorated. A pleasant place with a lovely garden. All rooms have central air-conditioning and bath or shower. 208 rooms.

Forum
Via Tor de'Conti 25, Rome
Telephone: 672–446
> A beautifully decorated hotel with a spectacular view overlooking the Trajan Forum and within walking distance of

the Colosseum. The rooms are somewhat small, but the atmosphere is pleasant and the service is excellent. 60 rooms.

Valadier
Via Della Fontanella 15, Rome
Telephone: 686–966

A distinguished small hotel with modern décor. Although situated next to the Piazza del Popolo in the commercial center of town, it's a quiet place. 40 rooms.

Second-class

Inghilterra
Via Bocca di Leone 14, Rome
Telephone: 689–010

This is an attractive small hotel with an old-fashioned atmosphere. Well-located near the Spanish Steps. Many rooms with balcony and bath. A very good buy. 90 rooms.

Panama
Via Salaria 336, Rome
Telephone: 867–060

This is a new building with an old-fashioned décor. Situated near the fashionable Parioli district, it's a small quiet hotel, and a 15-minute walk from the center of town. 45 rooms.

Sporting
Via Civinini 46, Rome
Telephone: 804–041

This newly built, modern steel and glass hotel is situated in the residential Parioli district. The rooms are rather small, but the rates are reasonable. All rooms come with bath or shower, and some are air-conditioned. 190 rooms.

Tiziano
Corso Vittorio Emanuele 110, Rome
Telephone: 655–087

This old-fashioned hotel is situated in the old city by the Corso road and near St. Peter's. Almost all rooms have baths. 50 rooms.

Hotels in Florence

Deluxe

Villa Medici
Via del Prato 42, Florence
Telephone: 261–331

One of the most sumptuous hotels located in the old center of Florence. The interior of this former villa is beautifully decorated. Swimming pool and air-conditioning. 105 rooms.

Excelsior-Italia
Piazza Ognissanti 3, Florence
Telephone: 294–301
> Many rooms have a lovely view overlooking the Arno River. Others overlook Borgo Ognissanti, a picturesque view of the Cathedral and the Tower of Giotto. Lovely suites. Air-conditioning. 215 rooms.

Grand Hotel
Piazza Ognissanti, Florence
Telephone: 294–401
> Many rooms in this elegant hotel have a balcony and a view of the Arno. Complete air-conditioning. 150 rooms.

First-class

Hotel De la Ville
Piazza Antinori 1, Florence
Telephone: 261–805
> Conveniently located off the fashionable Via Tornabuoni. A modern hotel with good-sized and well-furnished air-conditioned rooms. Excellent duplex for family of four. 85 rooms.

Villa La Massa
Candeli (4 miles from Florence)
> Beautifully situated near the Arno in a garden and countryside setting. Rooms are comfortable, clean, and well-furnished.

Second-class

Berchielli
Lungarno Acciaioli 14, Florence
Telephone: 21–530
> Located with a view of the Arno and near the Ponte Vecchio. Quiet, charming, nicely furnished rooms. 81 rooms. An excellent buy.

Continentale
Lungarno Acciaioli 2, Florence
Telephone: 282–392
> Well-located near the Ponte Vecchio and the center of town. An air-conditioned hotel with small but cheerful rooms. Attractive roof garden.

Villa Belvedere
Via B Castelli 3, Florence
Telephone: 222–501
> A pleasant hotel with a lovely view of Florence from across the Arno. 8 minutes from the center of town by car. This is a renovated villa with gardens and swimming pool. 30 rooms. Open only March through November.

Villa Azalee
Via le Fratelli 44, Florence
> Located away from the center of town, near Cascine Park. Well-furnished rooms, high ceilings, and a lovely place to relax if you don't have to be right in the center of things.

Pension (first-class)

Beacci
Via Tornabuoni 3, Florence
Telephone: 272–645
> Located on three floors above an art gallery. Well-maintained, comfortable, and liked by Americans. 29 rooms, most with bath. About $11 with meals.

What to Know Before You Go

"How Much Is That, Anyway?"

Understanding the money in Italy is simpler task than in many other countries. There is only one basic unit of currency, the lira. It comes in nine different denominations: five in coins, and four in paper money.

The coins are issued in sums of 5, 10, 20, 50, and 100 lire. Paper money comes in units of 500, 1000, 5000, and 10,000 lire.

The only difficulty with Italian money is that you will be dealing with large numbers when translating lire into dollars. It takes approximately 620 lire to equal one U.S. dollar (577 for one Canadian dollar). Transactions involving thousands of lire are common occurrences. An easy thing to remember is that 100 lire = 16¢, 1,000 lire = $1.60, and 10,000 lire = $16.00. To help you convert large numbers into dollars, use the conversion table shown below.

$U.S.–LIRE	$U.S.–LIRE	$U.S.–LIRE	$U.S.–LIRE	$U.S.–LIRE
1 = 620	14 = 8,680	27 = 16,740	40 = 24,800	80 = 49,600
2 = 1,240	15 = 9,300	28 = 17,360	41 = 25,420	90 = 55,800
3 = 1,860	16 = 9,920	29 = 17,980	42 = 26,040	100 = 62,000
4 = 2,480	17 = 10,540	30 = 18,600	43 = 26,660	110 = 68,200
5 = 3,100	18 = 11,160	31 = 19,220	44 = 27,280	120 = 74,400
6 = 3,720	19 = 11,780	32 = 19,840	45 = 27,900	130 = 80,600
7 = 4,340	20 = 12,400	33 = 20,460	46 = 28,520	140 = 86,800
8 = 4,960	21 = 13,020	34 = 21,080	47 = 29,140	150 = 93,000
9 = 5,580	22 = 13,640	35 = 21,700	48 = 29,760	200 = 124,000
10 = 6,200	23 = 14,260	36 = 22,320	49 = 30,380	250 = 155,000
11 = 6,820	24 = 14,880	37 = 22,940	50 = 31,000	300 = 186,000
12 = 7,440	25 = 15,500	38 = 23,560	60 = 37,200	400 = 248,000
13 = 8,060	26 = 16,120	39 = 24,180	70 = 43,400	500 = 310,000

Who and How to Tip

Tipping correctly is simply doing the "right thing," based on local customs. It's a nice way to say "thank you" to someone who has served you well. By following the guidelines in this section, you will be tipping on the same basis as the people who live in Rome and Florence.

HOTELS: A service charge of from 12% to 21% will be added to your hotel bill. In addition to this sum, leave a tip for the maid (300 to 500 lire), the hall porter (300 to 500 lire), and the concierge. The concierge should receive 10% of his charges if they are collected separately from the room bill when you leave. If the concierge does not bill you separately for telephone calls, postage, or other "helpful" services he may have rendered, give him from 1000 to 1500 lire. Should your stay at the hotel be a short one, say for two or three days, tip at the lower end of each range mentioned. If your stay is five days or longer, and the service is good, tip at the higher end.

PORTERS: Porters at train stations and the airport expect 200 lire for the first bag, and 100 lire for each additional piece of luggage. Hotel porters should get 100 lire per bag.

TAXIS: Tip 10% of the bill. Never leave less than 50 lire.

RESTAURANTS: A service charge of from 10% to 15% will be added to your bill. In addition to this sum, leave an extra tip if the service pleases you. The "something extra" should be about 10% of the bill, excluding the service charge.

COFFEE BARS: When drinking coffee while standing up at the bar, leave 10 lire per person. If you're being served at the table, leave 10% of the bill.

BARBER SHOPS: Give 200 lire as a tip to the person who served you; leave a little more (250 lire) if you're delighted.

HAIRDRESSERS: When you're through, take 12% of the total bill and distribute it among those who served you. Of the total, the manicurist gets 200 lire; the girl who washed your hair also gets 200 lire. What's left goes to the hairdresser.

"But Will It Fit?"

Generally speaking, clothing and shoe sizes are not the same throughout the world. While nothing replaces trying it on, the following comparisons will help you buy what fits:

WOMEN'S SIZES

Dresses & Coats			Blouses & Sweaters		
American	English	Continental	American	English	Continental
10	32	38	34	36	42
12	33	40	36	38	44
14	35	42	38	40	46
16	36	44	40	42	48
18	38	46	42	44	50
20	39	48	44	46	52

Ladies' Shoes				Stockings	
American	English	French	Italian	American & English	Continental
4–4½	2–2½	36	32	8	20¼ or 0
5–5½	3–3½	37	34	8½	21½ or 1
6–6½	4–4½	38	36–37	9	22¾ or 2
7–7½	5–5½	39	38–39	9½	24 or 3
8–8½	6–6½	40	40–41	10	25¼ or 4
9	7	41	42	10½	26½ or 5
9½–10	7½–8	42	43–44	11	27¾ or 6
				11½	29 or 7

MEN'S SIZES

Suits & Overcoats

American & English	Continental
36	46
38	48
40	50
42	52
44	54
46	56

Shirts

American & English	Continental
14	36
14½	37
15	38
15½	39
16	41
16½	42
17	43

Men's Shoes

American & English	Continental
7	40
7½	41
8–8½	42
9–9½	43
10–10½	44
11–11½	45

Men's Socks

American & English	Continental
9	37–38
9½	38–39
10	39–40
10½	40–41
11	41–42
11½	42–43

Men's Hats

American	English	Continental
6⅝	6½	53
6¾	6⅝	54
6⅞	6¾	55
7	6⅞	56
7⅛	7	57
7¼	7⅛	58
7⅜	7¼	59
7½	7⅜	60
7⅝	7½	61

Men's Sweaters

American	English	Continental
small	34	44
medium	36–38	46–48
large	40	50
X large	42–44	52–54

Gloves

Sizes are the same everywhere

CHILDREN'S SIZES

There is no accurate comparative size chart for children's clothing. On the continent, the sizing of children's clothing is inconsistent, and varies with each manufacturer. So if you're thinking of buying clothing abroad for a child, take a few simple measurements with you.

For a boy: his height alone is sufficient.

For a girl: her height is important; but if you have a dress at home that's the right size, measure its width across the shoulders and its length from neck to hemline.

"What's It Like Outside?"

It might help you to plan your wardrobe if you know in advance what the weather will be like in Rome and Florence at different times of the year. Bear in mind that the figures shown are averages, that Rome and Florence like every other city can be unseasonably warm or cold. Generally, the weather tends to be milder than in many parts of the United States and Canada.

IN ROME

Temperature	Jan.	Feb.	Mar.	Apr.	May	June
High	53°	55°	59°	66°	74°	82°
Average	45°	48°	52°	58°	65°	72°
Low	38°	40°	44°	49°	55°	62°
No. of Rainy Days	10	10	9	9	8	5

IN FLORENCE

Average Temperature	40°	45°	50°	57°	65°	73°

IN ROME

Temperature	July	Aug.	Sept.	Oct.	Nov.	Dec.
High	88°	87°	81°	70°	61°	53°
Average	78°	77°	73°	62°	54°	47°
Low	67°	66°	63°	54°	47°	40°
No. of Rainy Days	2	3	6	11	12	12

IN FLORENCE

Average Temperature	78°	76°	69°	59°	50°	41°

The Holidays of Italy

Italy abounds in religious and national holidays. Plan to do outdoor sightseeing or relax on these days when all the shops are closed:

New Year's Day
January 6 (Epiphany)
February 11 (Anniversary of concordat with the Vatican)
March 19 (St. Joseph)
Easter Sunday and Monday
April 25 (Liberation Day, World War II)
May 1 (Labor Day)
June 2 (Republic Day)
June 29 (Sts. Peter and Paul)
August 15 (Assumption)
November 1 (All Saints' Day)

November 4   (Victory Day)
December 8   (Immaculate Conception)
December 25, 26 (Christmas)

What to Do in Case of Emergency

Italy has a simple system to provide assistance to any person faced with an emergency. Just *telephone 113 from anywhere in Italy and help will be on its way.* Should your car break down, or should you become involved in an automobile accident, *telephone 116 for roadside aid.*

One word of caution: The pay telephones in Italy do not accept coins; they take only special slugs which can be purchased for 50 lire at any hotel or coffee bar. Buy one of these slugs in advance and carry it with you. With this slug in hand and by keeping telephone numbers 113 and 116 in mind, you will be ready for any emergency that may arise.

Have a safe journey!

Doctor: Ask the concierge at your hotel for the name of a reliable doctor. If you prefer a clinic, one run by English-speaking nuns is Ospedale di S. Stefano in Rotundo, Via Santo Stefano in Rotundo 6, telephone: 752–441.

Emergency Medical Care:

You may receive free treatment, including X-rays, at any hospital which has emergency service—*pronto soccorso*—if you come within 12 hours after an accident. Ask your concierge or the police for the nearest *pronto soccorso*.

Medicines and Prescriptions:

Robert's, Via del Corso 418 (English-speaking), Rome
Carlo Erba, Via del Corso 145 (open day and night), Rome
Farmacia Internazionale, Via Veneto 129, Rome
Silvestre, Piazza Di Spagna, Rome
Robert's, Via Tornabuoni 97, Florence

Lost and Found:

In Rome, telephone 572–189
In Florence, telephone 260–741

Legal Problems: Contact your Embassy or Consulate.

United States
Via Veneto 119, Telephone 4674, Rome
Lungarno Vespucci 38, Telephone 298–276, Florence
Canadian
Via G. B. de Rossi 27, Telephone 855–341, Rome

Airlines:

Pan American, Via San Nicola da Tolentino 77, Rome
TWA, Via Barberini 59–67, Rome
Canadian Pacific, Via Veneto 28, Rome
Alitalia, Via Bissolati, Rome

Shipping:
   Salviati and Santori, Via dei Quatro Venti, Rome
   (Ask for Mr. Russo who speaks English)
   Salviati and Santori, Via Zambertesgr 11,
      Telephone 263–341, Florence
   Messeri, Ltd., Piazza Strozzi 1, Telephone 23–524, Florence
Baby-Sitting Service:
   La Cicogna, Via Frattina 138, Telephone 686–909, Rome
   Villa "La Torrossa," Via B. da Maiano 3,
      Telephone 59–518, Florence
Miscellaneous:
   American Express, Piazza Di Spagna 38, Rome
      Via Tornabuoni 14R, Florence
   Thomas Cook and Son, Via Veneto 9–11, Rome
   Italian Tourist Office, Via Marghera 2, Rome
                          Via Tornabuoni 15, Florence

Crossing the Language Barrier

Italians are as complimented as any other people when a visitor shows enough interest in their country to pick up a few words in their language. Conversely, from the visitor's own point of view, a very rudimentary vocabulary is practically a necessity, because relatively few Italians talk much English. Here, to help you across the language barrier, are a few key words and phrases:

English	Italian
Do you speak English?	*Parla lei Inglese?*
Yes.—No.	*Si.—No.*
Excuse me.	*Scusi.*
Hello *(during the day)*.	*Buon giorno.*
Hello *(during the evening)*.	*Buona sera.*
Good-bye.	*Addio.*
So long.	*Ciao.* (pronounced: chow)
How are you?	*Come sta?*
Please give me . . .	*La prego mi dia . . .*
Thank you.	*Grazie.*
You're welcome.	*Prego.*
Please.	*Per piacere.*
Where?	*Dove?*
I don't understand.	*Non capisco.*
How much?	*Quanto?*
Too much.	*Troppo.*
All right.	*Bene.*
One, two, three, four,	*Uno, due, tre, quattro,*
five, six, seven, eight,	*cinque, sei, sette, otto,*
nine, ten, eleven, twelve,	*nove, dieci, undici, dodici,*
twenty, thirty, forty,	*venti, trenta, quaranta,*
fifty, one hundred	*cinquanta, cento*

Using this limited vocabulary and plenty of Italian sign language—constant gesturing with the hands—you're ready to approach almost any situation. *Buona fortuna* (good luck).

How to Use *Rome-Florence Discovery*

1. Please sign your *Rome-Florence Discovery* Courtesy Card at the time you detach it. Keep it with you, as it is not transferable.

2. The establishments described in this book have all agreed to extend special privileges to persons presenting the *Rome-Florence Discovery* Card. In restaurants and nightclubs, this privilege will take the form of a *cortesia*—an hors d'œuvre, a drink before or after your meal, a dessert or wine. The *cortesia*, which is indicated in the description, is at the discretion of the management. In other establishments, the privilege is a cash discount. All places are eager to welcome and serve you, and all maintain a policy of fixed prices.

3. Courtesy privileges in restaurants and nightclubs will be extended to four people together whether or not related by blood or marriage. Larger groups *must* be members of the same immediate family. Specific restrictions of this nature are indicated in association with the description of the appropriate establishments. In all other cases, the number of persons who may use one *Rome-Florence Discovery* Card is at the discretion of the establishment, and is governed by the rule of reason.

4. To obtain your *cortesia* in a restaurant or nightclub, please present your *Rome-Florence Discovery* Card upon entering. In other types of establishments, present it at the time you receive your bill. You may be asked to countersign the bill or receipt, so be sure you have previously signed your *Rome-Florence Discovery* Card itself.

5. *Cortesias* and discounts will be granted in exchange for payment in Italian currency or traveler's checks acceptable to the individual restaurant or other establishment. Credit cards are NOT accepted in conjunction with a *Rome-Florence Discovery* Card.

6. Discount privileges may not apply on reduced-price sale merchandise in shops, and advance notice need not be given.

7. Discount privileges do not apply to postage and mailing services, nor to taxes, if any.

8. The copyright holders of *Rome-Florence Discovery* have signed *cortesia* and discount-privilege agreements in good faith with each restaurant and other establishment, but cannot guarantee that these privileges will always be honored. If privileges are not honored by any establishment, please notify

    Discoveries Overseas, Inc.
    P.O. Box 2028
    Detroit, Michigan 48231 U.S.A.

9. Neither Discoveries Overseas, Inc., nor the authors, nor the copyright holders of *Rome-Florence Discovery,* nor the publisher, nor the seller of *Rome-Florence Discovery* shall be held responsible for any losses or injuries sustained in the premises of any establishment described herein, or as a result of any trade with these establishments.

Rome

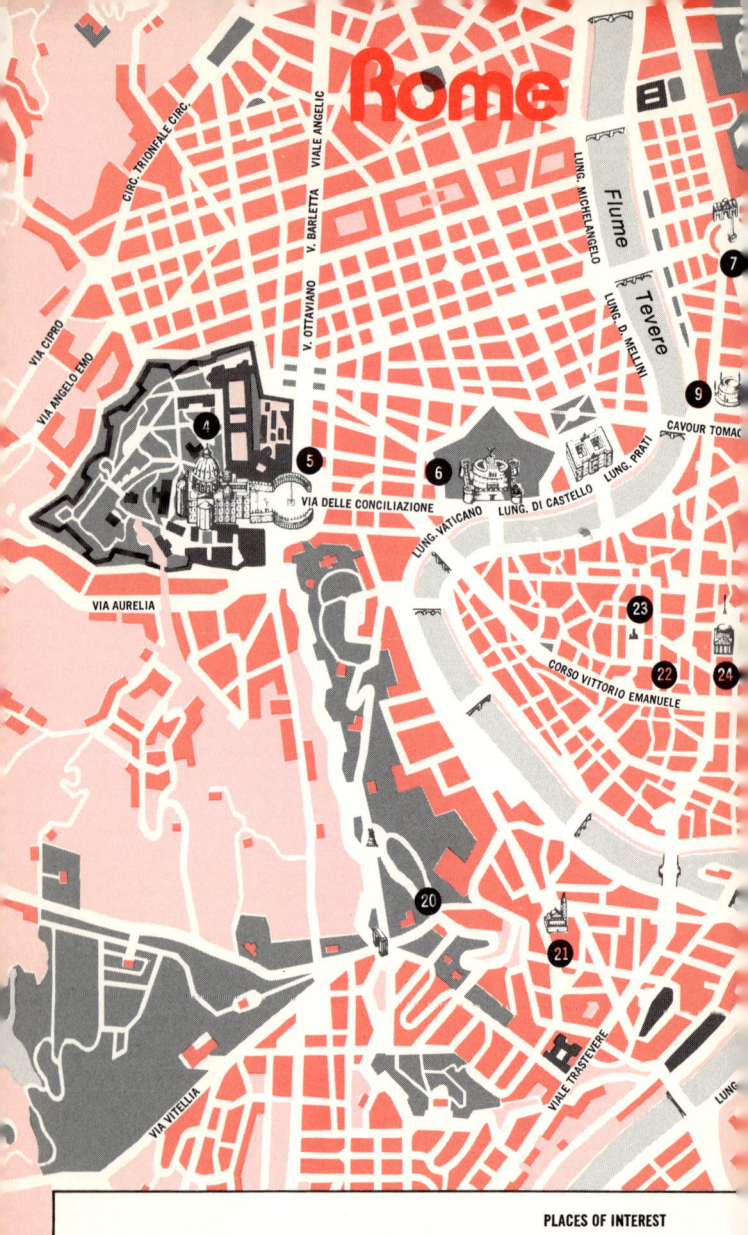

PLACES OF INTEREST

1. Museum in the Villa Giulia
2. National Gallery for Modern Art
3. Borghese Museum and Gallery
4. Vatican Museum
5. Saint Peter's Basilica
6. Castel Sant' Angelo (Hadrian's Tomb, Art-weapons collection)
7. Piazza del Popolo
8. Spanish Steps and Church SS. Trinita dei Monti
9. Tomb of Augustus
10. Primary Shopping District
11. Church S. Lorenzo in Lucina
12. National Gallery of Ancient Art in Palazzo Barberini
13. Santa Maria della Concezione
14. Gallery of the Academy of S. Luca
15. Trevi Fountain
16. Gallery Colonna
17. Terme Museum of Ancient Art (Museo Nazionale Romano)
18. Opera House
19. Central Railway (Termini Statio
20. Paolina Founta
21. Church of Sant
22. Museum of the Municipal Muse
23. Piazza Navonna
24. Pantheon
25. Prehistoric and Museum
26. Piazza Venezia

Inset street names:
- V. Bocca di Leone
- Via del Corce
- Via delle Carozzi
- P.za di Spagna
- Via del Corso
- Via Condotti
- Via Borgognona
- Via Frattina
- Via Della Vite
- Via Due Macelli

Map streets:
- VIA XX SETTEMBRE
- VIA QUIRINALE
- VIA NAZIONALE
- V. XXIV MAGGIO
- VIALE REGINA ELENA
- VIA MARSALA
- VIA GIOVANNI GIOLITTI
- VIA NOVEMBRE
- VIA DEI FORI IMPERIALI
- VIA MERULANA
- VIA LABICANA
- V. S. GIOVANNI IN LATERANO
- V. MANZONI
- VIALE AVENTINO
- VIA DELLE TERME
- VIA GALLIA
- VIA ETRURI
- VIA DI P.ta S. SEBASTIANO
- VIA APPIA ANTIC.

27. Monument to Vittorio Emanuele II
28. Capitoline Hill with Museum on the Piazza Campidoglio
29. Temple of Vesta
30. Basilica of S. Maria Maggiore
31. Colosseum
32. Porta San Paolo
33. Pyramid of Cestius
34. Basilica of S. Giovanni in Laterno
35. Baths of Caracalla

stevere

n Art

PLACES OF INTEREST

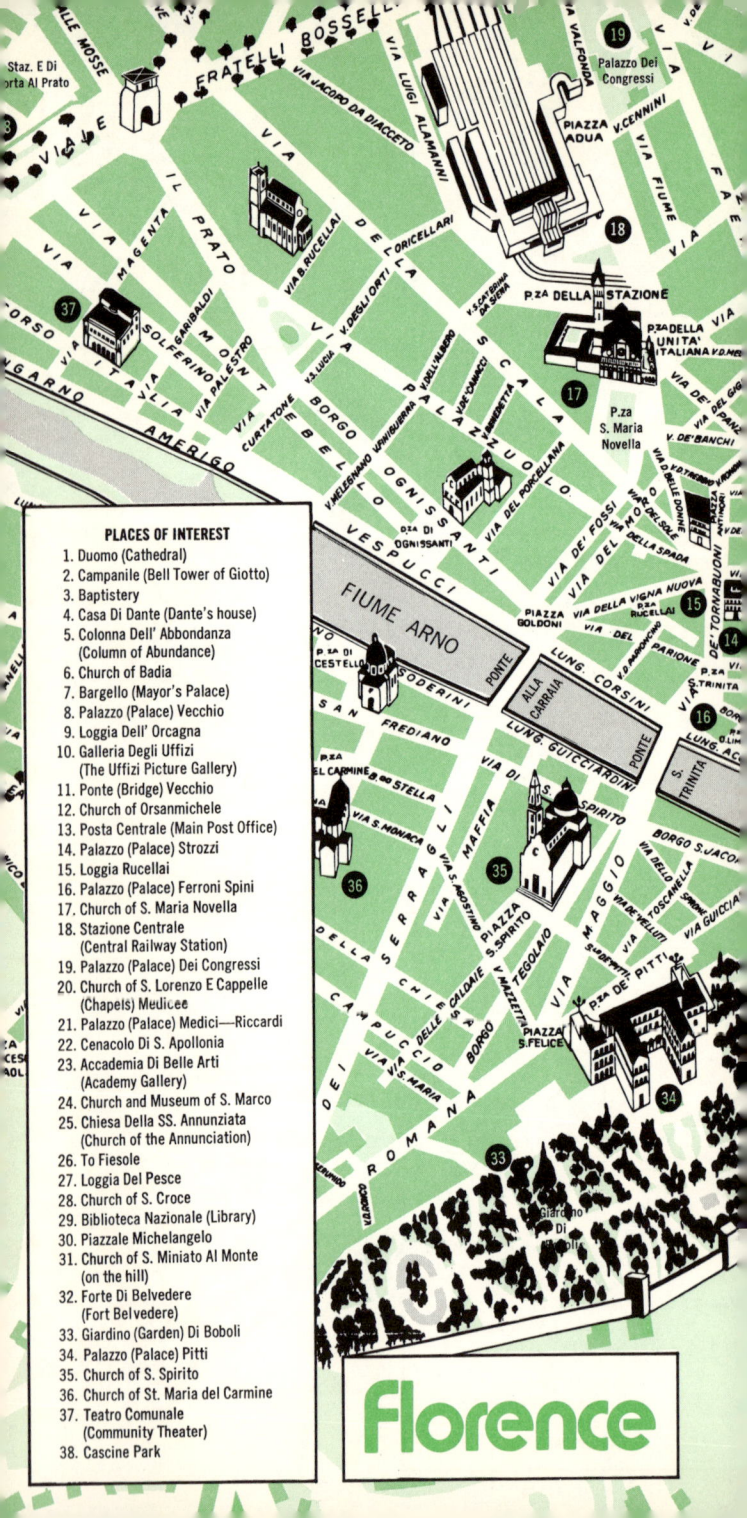

1. Duomo (Cathedral)
2. Campanile (Bell Tower of Giotto)
3. Baptistery
4. Casa Di Dante (Dante's house)
5. Colonna Dell' Abbondanza (Column of Abundance)
6. Church of Badia
7. Bargello (Mayor's Palace)
8. Palazzo (Palace) Vecchio
9. Loggia Dell' Orcagna
10. Galleria Degli Uffizi (The Uffizi Picture Gallery)
11. Ponte (Bridge) Vecchio
12. Church of Orsanmichele
13. Posta Centrale (Main Post Office)
14. Palazzo (Palace) Strozzi
15. Loggia Rucellai
16. Palazzo (Palace) Ferroni Spini
17. Church of S. Maria Novella
18. Stazione Centrale (Central Railway Station)
19. Palazzo (Palace) Dei Congressi
20. Church of S. Lorenzo E Cappelle (Chapels) Medicee
21. Palazzo (Palace) Medici—Riccardi
22. Cenacolo Di S. Apollonia
23. Accademia Di Belle Arti (Academy Gallery)
24. Church and Museum of S. Marco
25. Chiesa Della SS. Annunziata (Church of the Annunciation)
26. To Fiesole
27. Loggia Del Pesce
28. Church of S. Croce
29. Biblioteca Nazionale (Library)
30. Piazzale Michelangelo
31. Church of S. Miniato Al Monte (on the hill)
32. Forte Di Belvedere (Fort Belvedere)
33. Giardino (Garden) Di Boboli
34. Palazzo (Palace) Pitti
35. Church of S. Spirito
36. Church of St. Maria del Carmine
37. Teatro Comunale (Community Theater)
38. Cascine Park

florence

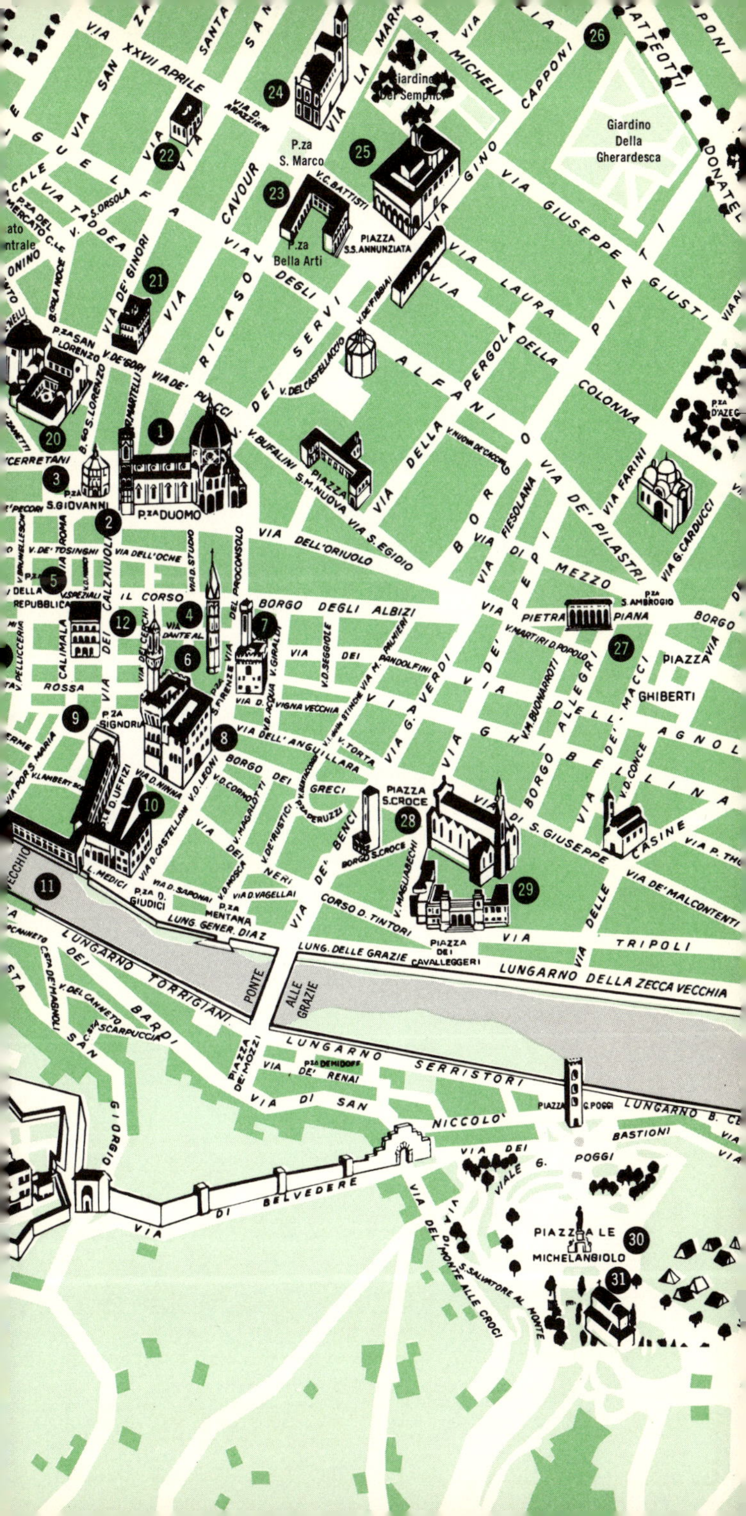
Via XXVII Aprile
Via Santa
Via San Gallo
Via Guelfa
Via La Marmora
P.za Micheli
Via Capponi
Via Matteotti
Giardino Dei Semplici
Giardino Della Gherardesca
P.za S. Marco
V.C. Battisti
Via Gino Capponi
Via Giuseppe Giusti
Via Cavour
Via D. Arazzieri
Via Taddea
V. S.Orsola
P.za del Mercato C.le
Piazza S.S.Annunziata
P.za Bella Arti
Via Laura
Via Ricasoli
Via degli Servi
V. de' Fibbiai
Via de' Ginori
Borgo la Noce
P.za San Lorenzo
V. de' Gori
Via de' Pucci
V. del Castellaccio
Via Alfani
Via della Pergola
Via della Colonna
Via Pinti
P.za D'Azeglio
B. S. Lorenzo
Via Martelli
Cerretani
P.za S.Giovanni
P.za Duomo
V. Bufalini
Piazza S.M.Nuova
Via della
V. Nuova de' Caccini
Borgo
Via Fiesolana
Via de' Pilastri
Via Farini
Via G. Carducci
Pecori
Via Roma
V. de' Tosinghi
Calzaiuoli
Via dell'Oche
Via D. Studio
Via del Proconsolo
Via dell'Oriuolo
Via S. Egidio
Via di Mezzo
V. della Repubblica
V. Speziali
Il Corso
Borgo degli Albizi
Via de' Pepi
Via Pietrapiana
P.za S. Ambrogio
Borgo
Calimala
Via dei Cerchi
Via Dante Al.
Via D. Seggiole
Via dei Pandolfini
Via M. Palmieri
V. Giraldi
V. Martiri D. Popolo
Piazza Ghiberti
V. Pellicceria
Rossa
P.za Signoria
P.za S. Firenze
Via D. Acqua
Vigna Vecchia
V. Stinche
Via Verdi
Via de'
V.M. Buonarroti
Borgo Allegri
Via dei Macci
Via Ghibellina
Via dell'Agnolo
Terme
Via Por S. Maria
V. Lambertesca
Via D. Uffizi
Via D. Ninna
V.D. Leoni
Borgo dei Greci
Via dell'Anguillara
V. Torta
V.D. Cornio
V. Magalotti
V. de' Rustici
P.za Peruzzi
Via de' Benci
Piazza S.Croce
Borgo S.Croce
V. Magliabechi
Via di S. Giuseppe
Via delle Casine
V.D. Conce
Via P. Thouar
Via de' Malcontenti
Via D. Castellani
Vecchio
L. Medici
P.za D. Giudici
Via D. Saponai
V.D. Mosca
Via dei Neri
V. D. Vagellai
P.za Mentana
Lung. Gener. Diaz
Corso D. Tintori
Piazza dei Cavalleggeri
Via delle
Via Tripoli
Lung. delle Grazie
Lungarno della Zecca Vecchia
Lungarno Torrigiani
Ponte
Alle Grazie
Bardi
V. del Canneto
C.sta Scarpuccia
Piazza de' Mozzi
Lungarno Serristori
P.za Demidoff
Via de' Renai
Via di San Niccolò
Piazza G. Poggi
Lungarno B. Cellini
San Giorgio
Via di Belvedere
Via dei Bastioni
Viale G. Poggi
Via del Monte alle Croci
Via S. Salvatore al Monte
Piazzale Michelangiolo
1 2 3 4 5 6 7 8 9 10 11 12
20 21 22 23 24 25 26 27 28 29 30 31

Index

Accademia, 28
airlines, 179
Angeletti (silver, jewelry), 111
Antico Caffè Greco (coffee bar), 32–33
antiques, 129, 130, 133–136
Appian Line, The (tours), 161–162
Appian Way, 24–25
Archimede, Trattoria (restaurant), 56
Arch of Constantine, 22–23
Arco di S. Calisto (restaurant), 50
Arno, River, 19, 26
Artestile (china), 115
art galleries 129–131

baby-sitters, 180
Baptistery, 19, 26, 27
barbers, 140–143
Barber Shop (barber) 142
Bargello, 29
Bar La Borsa (coffee bar), 33
Barroccio, Il (restaurant), 60
Barzini, Luigi, 12
Basilica of St. John Lateran, 30
Baths of Caracalla, 21, 23, 30, 32
Beacci (hotel), 172
beaches, 33
Beatrice (women's wear), 75
Bellini, Luigi, Galleria (antiques), 135
Berchielli (hotel), 171
Bernini Fountain, 21
Black Bar, The (coffee bar), 33
Boboli Gardens, 27, 32
Boccuzzi (leather fashions), 100
books, rare, 129, 132
Borghese Gardens, 30, 34
Buca Lapi, Ristorante, 61
buses, 159–160

Cammillo, Trattoria (restaurant), 65
Campanile, 26
Capitoline Museum, 26
car rental, 163
Casa Dell' Alluminio (housewares), 116
Cassina (furniture), 117

catacombs, 24-25
Cavalieri Hilton (hotel), 169
Cecconi, Roberto (jewelry), 110
Cesarina (restaurant), 52
Chesne Dauphiné (antiques), 136
children's clothing, 72, 92, 177
china and crystal, 113–115
Church of Santa Croce, 29
Cicogna, La (children's clothing), 92
Cisterna, Ristorante la, 45
Clemente (leather goods), 95
clothing, shopping for, 72–104
clothing sizes, 176–177
Club Gattopardo (nightclub), 153
coffee bars, 31, 32–33, 151
Colosseum, 22, 23, 30, 31, 34
concerts, 32, 151
Continentale (hotel), 171
Coq d'Or, Le (nightclub), 156
Corner Shop, The (women's wear), 98
Cortesia, 6, 38, 182
cosmetology, 139–140, 145
Costa, Gino (leather goods), 85
currency, 175

Dante G. (hairdresser), 148
Dauphiné, Chesne (antiques), 136
Da Vinci, Leonardo, 18, 26
Davitti, Paola (women's wear), 97
De la Ville (hotel), 169
Del Bono, Giovanni (silver), 122
Dell' Alluminio, Casa (housewares), 116
Dell' Ariccia (leather goods), 82
Di Cori (gloves), 84
Discovery card, 6, 74, 182–183
doctors, 179
Duomo, Il, 26, 27
Dupre (leather goods), 93

emergencies, 179–180
Er Faciolaro (restaurant), 59
Etruscans, 26, 28
Euroselfdrive (car rental), 163

189

Excelsior (hotel), 169
Excelsior Italia (hotel), 170–171
Eyre & Humbert (sightseeing), 164

fabrics, 107, 125
Faciolaro, Er (restaurant), 59
Femme Sistina (hairdresser, cosmetologist), 145
Fiesole, 28
Filippo (hairdresser), 146
Flea Market, 31, 129
floods, 17, 19, 20
Florence, 17–20, 26–29
Fontinalia (jewelry), 112
foods, description of, 39–42
Forum (hotel), 169–170
Fra Angelico, 18, 29
Fragiacomo (shoes), 88
Francesco Navone (table linens), 123
furniture, 107, 117, 118

Galileo (Galilei), 18, 19, 26, 29
Galleria Aldo Soligo (antiques), 133
Galleria Luigi Bellini (antiques), 135
Gattopardo, Club (nightclub), 153
George Lester Gallery (art), 129
Ghiberti Brothers, 19, 26, 27, 29
Giannino in S. Lorenzo (restaurant), 62
Giggi Fazi (restaurant), 62
Gino Costa (leather goods), 85
Giotto (di Bondone), 18, 26, 27, 29
Giovanni Del Bono (silver), 122
Grand Hotel (hotel), 171
guide tours, 161–162, 164–166

Hadrian's Tomb, 25, 30
Hadrian's Villa, 25
hairdressers, 139–141, 144–146, 148
handicrafts, 107–109, 114, 126
Hassler Villa Medici (hotel), 169
Helio Cabala (restaurant), 54
holidays, 178
horse races, 33
Horti Galateae (restaurant), 55
Hotel De la Ville (hotel), 171

hotels, 168–172
hours for shopping, 72, 74
housewares, 116

Il Barroccio (restaurant), 60
Imperial Forum, 20, 30, 34
Inghilterra (hotel), 170

Janiculum Hill, 31
jewelry, 79, 80, 107–108, 110–112, 120, 121

La Cicogna (children's clothing), 92
La Medusa (art), 131
La Tazza d'Oro (coffee bar), 33
Laurentis, Dino de, 14
Leather goods, 73, 74, 82–85, 93–96, 100, 108
Le Coq d'Or (nightclub), 156
Le Coq d'Or (restaurant), 46
legal problems, 179
L'Escargot (restaurant), 47
Lester, George, Gallery (art), 129
Liberia Antiquaria Querzole (rare books), 132
linens, 107–108, 123, 124
Lorenzale (antiques), 134
Lo Scarabocchio (discothèque), 154
lost and found, 179
Luciana (jewelry), 79
Lydia de Roma (women's wear), 76

Machiavelli, Niccolo, 18, 19, 26, 29
Madova Gloves, 96
marble, 107, 112
Marcello Prageldi (men's-wear), 91
medical care, 179
Medici family, 18–19, 26–29
Medici-Riccardi Palace, 27, 28
Medusa, La (art), 131
men's-wear, 71–72, 85–91, 100–104, 177
Michelangelo (Buonarroti), 18, 19, 22, 24, 26, 28, 29
Miranda (women's wear), 78
Mondialtur (sightseeing), 161–162
Moscardi (woodcarving), 126

movie industry, 11, 14, 32
Myricae (handicrafts), 114

Navone, Francesco (table linens), 123
Neuber, H. (men's-wear), 104
night life, 151–156
Nucci (jewelry), 80

Obelisco Gallery (art), 129
Odyssia Gallery (art), 129
opera, 151
Otello, Ristorante, 66

Palazzi (men's-wear), 89
Pallazzo, Vecchio, 28
Panama (hotel), 170
Pantheon, 23, 25, 30
Paoli, Ristorante, 63
Paola Davitti (women's wear), 97
Parco dei Principi (hotel), 169
Passetto, Ristorante, 44
Pasticceria Rosati (coffee bar), 33
Peluso (men's-wear), 90
Peppino (barber), 143
Persepolis (carpets), 119
phrases, 141, 180–181
Piattelli (men's, women's clothing), 86
Piazza del Campidoglio, 22
Piazza della Signoria, 28
Piazza Navona, 21
Piazza Venezia, 22, 30
Piccini Fratelli (jewelry), 121
Piero, Restaurant da, 68
Piper Club (nightclub), 155
Pitti Palace, 27, 28
Ponte Vecchio, 19, 26, 108, 120–122
population, 12, 26
Porta Portese, 31, 129
Prageldi, Marcello (men's-wear), 91

Raphael (hotel), 169
Raphael's (leather goods), 83
Raspini (shoes), 102
Re degli Amici (restaurant), 57
Restaurant da Piero, 68
Ricami di Firenze (lingerie), 99
Risaliti, A. (jewelry), 120
Ristorante Buca Lapi, 61
Ristorante la Cisterna, 45

Ristorante Otello, 66
Ristorante Paoli, 63
Ristorante Passetto, 44
Ristorante Valle "La Biblioteca," 49
Rivoire (coffee bar), 33
Roberto Cecconi (jewelry), 110
Roman Forum, 22, 30
Romano (shoes), 103
Rome, 11–17, 21–26, 30–34
Romolo (restaurant), 58

Sabatini in Trastevere (restaurant), 51
St. John Lateran Basilica, 30
St. Peter's Basilica, 23, 24, 30
Sanna (shoes), 87
Santa Croce, Church of, 29
Santa Maria della Concezione, 25–26
Santa Maria Novella (church), 28
Scarabocchio, Lo (discothèque), 154
Schneider Gallery (art), 129
shipping, 179–180
shoes, 87, 88, 102, 103, 176, 177
shopping, clothes, 71–104
shopping for the home, 107–109, 111–119, 121–124, 126
shopping streets, 72–74, 108, 129–130
sightseeing, 21–34, 159–166
silver, 107, 108, 111, 121, 122
Sistine Chapel, 24
soccer, 31
Soligo, Aldo Galleria (antiques), 133
Sostanza Trattoria (restuarant), 64
Sound and Light, 151–152
Spagnol, L. (women's wear), 77
Spanish Steps, 21, 30
Spartaco and Ugo (hairdresser), 144
Sporting (hotel), 170
SPQR, 13
Spulcioni, C. (leather goods), 94
streetcars, 159–160
strikes, 14, 15
Studio Room (women's wear), 76
subway, 160

191

TAF (linens, lingerie), 124
taxis, 159
Tazza d'Oro, La (coffee bar), 33
Tecno (furniture), 118
The Appian Line (tours), 161–162
The Corner Shop (women's wear), 98
13 Gobbì (restaurant), 67
tipping, 175–176
Tivoli, 25
Tiziano (hotel), 170
Tomassini (lingerie), 81
Trastevere, 31, 45, 50–51, 58, 129
Trattoria Cammillo (restaurant), 65
Trattoria Archimede (restaurant), 56
Trattoria Sostanza (restaurant), 64
Tre Scalini (coffee bar), 33
Trevi Fountain, 29, 30
Trotta Wigs (wigs), 147

Uffizi Galleries, 29

Umberto Zanobetti (men's, women's wear), 101
University of Rome, 13

Valadier (hotel), 170
Valle "La Biblioteca," Ristorante, 49
Valli (fabrics), 125
Vatican, 11, 13, 15, 16, 23, 24
Victor Emmanuel Monument, 22
Villa Azalee (hotel), 171
Villa Belvedere (hotel), 171
Villa Borghese, 25
Villa dei Cesari, La (restaurant), 53
Villa d'Este, 25
Villa La Mossa (hotel), 171
Villa Medici (hotel), 170

weather, 178
wigmaker, 147
WMF (tableware), 113
women's wear, 71–81, 86–88, 97–103, 176

Zanobetti, Umberto (men's, women's wear), 101